THE PERFECT GIFT

WRITTEN BY

Chris Gore and Angela Locke

Special thanks to Jaymin, Charlotte, & David for having your smiles featured on the cover.

Cover by Jonathan Bärnreuther & Valory Immel | http://valoryevalyn.com

Website: www.chrisgore.org

Email: ThePerfectGiftProject@gmail.com

ISBN: 978-1-64255-595-0

Printed in Canada

SEEDING A BOOK

We trust that you will be filled with hope and encouragement as you read *The Perfect Gift*. Our heart's desire and goal is that worldwide, every parent or grandparent of a child with special needs would receive a copy of this writing for free.

We invite you to partner with us to make this ambitious goal possible by purchasing a book on behalf of those families. We would be able to put this in the hands of families anywhere in the world for an average $34.95 USD per book (which includes shipping).

For questions or to join us in this exciting endeavor, please email us or send your gift directly, noting it as "Seeding a book," to the following PayPal address: ThePerfectGiftProject@gmail.com

With much love,

www.chrisgore.org

DEDICATION

I want to first dedicate this book to my wonderful team that gave many hours to this project to bring hope and encouragement to families all over the world. I love and appreciate each of you and this amazing project could not have happened without your incredible help!

Angela Locke, who works for me and is a Pastor for children with special needs, relentlessly went after this project, interviewing families and following up on their stories. Without your help, Angela, *The Perfect Gift* would have been a few more years away. I am eternally grateful for not only the hard work that you put into this book, but also the amazing heart that you poured out making this happen!

My third-year student, Jonathan Bärnreuther, who gave many volunteer hours designing all of the graphic art and layout of *The Perfect Gift*.

Dave Arns who freely gave his time to edit my poor grammar and make me look like a genius.

Also, of great importance to me, is to dedicate this book to all of the parents of children with special needs. You are my heroes and it's an incredible privilege to meet you from all over the world. It is my honor to love, hug, and minister to you and your children and assure you that it's all going to work out. We are on the winning side! I also want to especially recognize the families who shared their stories with us. Thank you for your vulnerability and courage in sharing with the world what Jesus has done in your lives. As others read this and experience breakthrough in their own lives, know that their testimonies are also a part of your family's legacy.

Last, but certainly not least, I dedicate this book to my daughter Charlotte and the rest of the children and adults with special needs. You are seen. You are known. You are valued. You are loved. You are important. You are our friends. You are the faces of revival! The testimony of Jesus is the spirit of prophecy. May this writing prophesy to the completion of your healing as you step into the fullness of all that Jesus paid for!

ANGELA LOCKE BIOGRAPHY

Angela Locke is originally from Ohio, where she worked for nine years at a children's hospital before moving to Redding, California. During her five years in Redding, she was on staff at Bethel Church as the special-needs pastor, where she and her team cultivated an atmosphere for children with special needs to be known, valued, loved, and empowered, with an emphasis on healing breakthrough.

She was also on staff under Chris Gore in the Healing Rooms as the children's team leader. It was her great joy to lead, equip, empower, and minister alongside of a team of passionate adults and sixty mighty children who ministered healing to the sick. She is a carrier of hope and has a passion for seeing all children walk in the fullness of their potential in Christ!

DEAR READER,

One of my greatest privileges has been to meet the heroes of life who are the parents of children with special needs. For many years, we have had a passion to see healing happen in the lives of these precious children, but soon realized that their parents also needed much encouragement as they go throughout their daily life. I was beginning to meet many parents who lived in shame and guilt and who had lost hope in God for the healing of their children. The heart of *The Perfect Gift* is to bring the truth of God's Word and much-needed encouragement to the incredible parents and caregivers of children with special needs. We want to help people see past the condition or diagnosis and instead see the identity of the child. We want to see families thriving and hope rekindled. Religion in itself is powerless and has fed us so many lies. As parents ourselves of a daughter with special needs, we have also had to address the hard questions and the critics. We have been through the fire and there are days we still feel its intensity. However, even in the heat of the fire, we can still thrive. Sometimes in life, we will only receive breakthrough when we can learn to rest in the fire.

Friends, we are living in a new day, a day where we are starting to see breakthrough in the lives of our precious children! It's time that we wash off powerless religion that would say not to get our hopes up and we embrace the power of the Gospel. It's time to see Jesus get what He paid for and to see healing and hope flow into our families!

I trust that you will be encouraged and infused with hope as you read the stories and teaching moments of *The Perfect Gift*.

With much love,

Chris Gore

THE PERFECT GIFT

Every good gift and every perfect gift is from above, and comes down from the Father of lights, with whom there is no variation or shadow of turning. James 1:17

There is no greater story to tell than the one that has been written by Jesus Christ. Before the very breath of God spoke light into existence, Jesus was there. His story began before the foundation of the world was created and it has never stopped. Over 2,000 years ago, the greatest gift we could ever be given came in the flesh in the form of Emmanuel–"God with us" and His name is Jesus. His greatest sacrifice was to give up His own life so that we could inherit life with Him. *We* were the joy set before Him. This book is about Jesus. Without Jesus, none of the stories you are about to read would have happened. He is our Healer and He is our Perfect Gift!

INTRODUCTION

As mentioned, the heart in writing this book is to bring encouragement, hope, and faith to those with special needs and to anyone who cares for them. We will primarily refer to parents in this writing, but know that if you value these precious ones, you too carry the heart of God for them, and this book is for you. Each person, whether disabled or not, is the absolute perfect gift from God. God is perfect, so He can only make perfect things. Likewise, He also restores things back to His original design, which is what we have seen happen time and time again with children with special needs. God has been and will always be the Healer. He first called Himself the "Lord who heals" in Exodus 15:26 and that hasn't changed, no matter what our circumstance. His Name is His nature and He forever covenanted to be our Healer through the death of His Son Jesus Christ.

Many of you may know that my wife Liz and I have three beautiful daughters–Charlotte, Emma, and Sophie. Our oldest daughter, Charlotte, was born in 1995 and has spastic quadriplegia with cerebral palsy. We've been on a journey her entire life of really understanding the heart of God towards healing and the heart of God towards her. Our journey with her is really what thrust me into the healing ministry and she has since taught us so much about patience, kindness, love, peace, perseverance, joy, and faith. In the process, we have discovered that to know God's heart towards healing and His heart towards Charlotte, we just need to look at the person of Jesus. Hebrews 1:3 says that Jesus is "the brightness of His [The Father's] glory and the express image of His person . . ." and then in John 14:9 Jesus states, "He who has seen Me has seen the Father." When we look at the person of Jesus, we recognize that He never put a condition or sickness on people to teach them a lesson and He never caused a storm. Instead, what we do see is that every sick and crippled person that ever came to Jesus was healed, without exception; every storm that He came into contact with, He calmed; and every funeral that He went to, He messed up; including His own! If Jesus is the exact representation of the Father, which He is, then the Father is like that too, and we can know for certain His heart towards our families and for healing.

One of the most difficult things is seeing so many parents of children with special needs that not only don't have faith, but they've also lost hope. There's so much torment in their homes and lives because of what they are going through. Believe me, our family has been there before. Last year, there was a time when Charlotte was having a really rough week. She was upset, cranky, would scream as soon as we sat her in her wheelchair, and needed to see the doctor multiple times. We thought that maybe one of the titanium rods in her back was broken, which would lead to another surgery. I was in a tailspin and could feel it affecting my peace. Pastor Kris Vallotton and I were talking and his words to me were literally life-changing. He said to me, "Chris, the storm may be around you, but it doesn't have to be in you." The revelation of Jesus in that simple sentence was all it took to help me find my peace again. The person of peace, Jesus, is always accessible in every believer. There's not a moment in life, no matter how difficult, that we lose access to that peace. That reality is available to you as well.

We want to begin this book by acknowledging how each person, whether disabled or not, is the perfect gift from God. When God formed us in our mother's wombs, we were made into His likeness and image, and He is perfect! What we have often seen is that the identity of the child and the child's condition have been viewed as one and the same, when in fact they are two separate things. Again, the child is the absolute, perfect gift from God. However, the condition that the child has is not. God cannot give us something that He Himself does not possess and God does not have a sickness or disability. What has happened is that, as a society and as parents, many of us are looking for peace and reconciliation as to why our children have a condition or sickness. So, we come to the conclusion that it's from God and that gives us some type of closure. This thinking does carry peace with it, but it's not the peace that God would give us; it's the peace of the world. We often make the identity of the child and the condition of the child one because of the lack of breakthrough that we have seen in this area. However, God doesn't want our children sick or with a disability. Please hear what I am not saying. I'm not saying that God does not love our children. He absolutely does and like any good Father, He wants the best for His children and to see them thrive. Don't we all?

We understand that in today's culture, not everyone believes that Jesus still heals today. To be honest, I have never faced so much resistance over any topic than what I have in desiring to see these children set free and healed. This book's intent is not to discuss the theology of healing, as there are a lot of great resources on that topic, including simply studying the life of Jesus in the Bible. Furthermore, as we have been intentional in praying for children with special needs, we've experienced that people can be particularly passionate about their differing perspectives and feelings. We find that those who disagree that healing can happen for children with disabilities can often come from a place of pain and disappointment or they just simply haven't understood our heart. However, in knowing the heart of the Father and in talking to families who have seen their children healed, the arguments go silent for us. To hear that a child who had never talked before, say "Mama" for the first time will forever change how you see things.

There is hope! When Jesus died on the cross, He took what we deserved so that we can receive what He deserved. Scripture tells us in John 10:10, "The thief [enemy] does not come except to steal, kill, and destroy. I [Jesus] have come that they may have life, and that they may have it more abundantly." Read this closely: God is not punishing you by afflicting your child with a disability. A good Father does not do that and His Son already took the only punishment required. There is absolutely nothing that you did wrong to cause this to happen. For those who may have experienced a more difficult past where your child was born with effects from drug abuse or other reasons, the blood of Jesus is still enough to change your past and your future. Let's believe Jesus for that abundant life! Abundant life for our children is one where they are free of seizures, spastic muscles, social isolation, and language barriers. Abundant life is where they can reach their fullest potential in God like anyone else and are free to run and dream. As of today, we've heard of fifty-three reports of full or significant breakthrough in children who were on the autism spectrum. Not all have been prayed for by me or even at Bethel Church, as the healing power of Jesus is available inside of every believer. Learn to recognize Him in the ones around you. Also, in the Kingdom of God, thanksgiving brings increase. With this in mind, we have intentionally highlighted both stories of children and adults who have been fully healed, as well as those who are still in process. These are their first-hand accounts.

We've then included some of our own insights into some keys for breakthrough and a place for reflection after each story. Every breakthrough is significant and Jesus deserves all the glory for every one of them! As you read their stories, begin to give thanks for what Jesus has done and may Holy Spirit ignite your faith and hope to see the Kingdom of God come in the life of your family in Jesus' Mighty Name!

CHAPTER 1

THE SEED OF HOPE

BRENDAN´S STORY

Like all testimonies, Brendan's is amazing but is unique in that from the day we got the first prophetic word that Brendan would be healed of autism, we had two years of hanging on to hope. We continued believing in God's goodness and faithfulness, believing in His promises even when our circumstances didn't line up, being steady and strong even when things seemed hopeless, and declaring the word of the Lord back to Him, saying, "But God, You said! You said my son would be healed. You said by Your Son's stripes we are healed." Brendan's faith, mixed with courage and persistence, landed him in front of Chris Gore late on the night of May 25, 2013 and when they prayed, autism bowed its knee to Jesus. Brendan had received prayer who knows how many times, but finally, we saw it break. He physically felt it leave his body. Love won that night! Love always does!

Brendan was born in June of 2003, and has been a part of our family ever since he was forty-five minutes old. We adopted him that day and it's hard to believe he's already fourteen! I previously had several pregnancy losses, including a thirty-seven-week stillbirth, and then the month before Brendan was born, I had another miscarriage. Although those experiences were difficult, he would never have joined our family had that not happened. Another beautiful thing that came out of our tragic losses was that I was able to breastfeed Brendan the day he was born. Although this was all great, Brendan's time in the womb had already been marked with a lot of chaos. According to the adoption agency, when his biological mom was twenty weeks pregnant, she went to have an abortion, but changed her mind when she saw that her baby was a boy. They also told us that she smoked, drank, used drugs, and was the victim of abuse during the pregnancy. So, Brendan entered our world with rejection and chaos already a part of his life, and he joined our family, in which I was still in need of physical and emotional healing myself.

I had been diagnosed with fibromyalgia and suffered with anxiety, suicidal thoughts, and depression. At eighteen, I began having panic attacks. At one point, I was even in a mental hospital where I told God that He either needed to show up, or that I was done. I had severe night terrors and spiritual attacks. One day, God woke me up in the middle of the night and spoke to me. I didn't hear the voice of the Lord a lot, so I knew this was significant. He said, "You have to get off of your medications. They are killing you." This made me panic even more because I was dependent on them. However, this began my two-year process of weaning myself off medications. During this time, I regularly had to

exchange lies for truth and continue to be persistent. The reason I share this part of my own journey is because I realized that as I got "my stuff" healed, Brendan started getting better too. If I didn't get healed up, but Brendan did, I wouldn't have known how to navigate his behaviors and help steward his healing. As parents, we need to let God touch every place in our own lives so we can be fully healthy and whole for our children.

So, as you can tell, when we adopted Brendan, my life had been marked with "hope deferred." My heart was still grieving. This was not the life that we had imagined. I bury a child and then finally adopt a child whom we love, but who is completely opposite to what we had imagined. Let me paint a picture of what life was like before Brendan was healed. He was a difficult baby and his childhood was filled with many diagnoses and twelve or thirteen surgeries before the age of nine. He was diagnosed with ADHD, fetal alcohol syndrome, sensory integration disorder, and moderate to severe autism. About 90% of the time, he would go into what we called "Brendan's World," where it was like he was somewhere else. He was very hyperactive and would be deeply immersed in whatever he was doing and completely unaware of and disconnected from the rest of the world. Sometimes, I would check on him in his room and he would never notice that I was there, even if I sat right next to him. He would not make eye contact and was totally inappropriate when it came to social interactions and sensory processing. It was a battle. We would be awakened by his intense night terrors in which many times, we'd have to strip him of all his clothes and put him in a cold shower to wake him up. His reality just wasn't our reality. His speech development was delayed and he also had an oral fixation where he would eat crayons as a kindergartener. His behavioral issues were severe. If he would hear a baby crying, he would want to punch it, and to our dismay, sometimes did. When he began school, I was always getting phone calls because he was really challenging for people to be around.

At the age of eight, this was part of his evaluation report:

Inventory for Client and Agency Planning (ICAP), Score/Level of 47/4, ABL III, overall age equivalence of 4 years, 2 months. Area of strength is personal livings skills. Area of greatest need is social/communication skills. Significant maladaptive behaviors present.

Childhood Autism Rating Scale, 2nd edition, High-Functioning (CARS-2-HF), Total Raw Score of 40.5, indicating that Brendan is experiencing severe symptoms of an Autism Spectrum Disorder.

In the beginning of 2011, we were faced with even more challenges. Brendan's eyes started crossing and rolling and we were told that he either had a brain tumor or was having seizures, which gratefully ended up not being the case. Then, he needed to have a hernia repair. In the midst of it all, I was also going through a massive detox from my medications. It was all very overwhelming. Little did we know that just two months from then, we would be given a seed of hope to grab on to: that one day Brendan would be healed. So, what if, in the face of all of this, we had not continued to press in? It was beyond stressful, but we kept asking ourselves, what is God doing and how does He want us to engage and respond despite our circumstances?

That seed of hope came in April of 2011 when Bonnie Chavda preached at our church. That weekend, they talked about Naaman from the Bible in 2 Kings 5. Naaman's healing of leprosy wasn't how he wanted it to look and he had to humble himself to receive it by dipping seven times in a river until he was healed. Every time we would take Brendan up for prayer, we felt like Naaman. Here we were, dipping again. Every time we would "dip" him and come up, the autism would still be there. It was a humiliating time. However, there was something in me that felt that if God did it for Naaman, He would do it for us. This story was a rhema word for us. Bonnie was giving away a CD and called out that it was to be given to "someone who has a child with a learning disability." As she gave it to me, she said that children have been healed from autism as they listened to it. We knew that this was a possible diagnosis for Brendan, but she didn't know that, and he ended up being officially diagnosed shortly thereafter. Bonnie didn't say much. She didn't pray a crazy, radical prayer. She didn't yell and scream at demons and command them to leave my son. She just released hope. She planted a seed that was bathed in the love of Christ. We chose to partner with the seed. We nourished it, we protected it, we believed in it, and it took root. That was the first time that I thought maybe Brendan could be healed.

It was beyond stressful, but we kept asking ourselves, what is God doing and how does He want us to engage and respond despite our circumstances?

During worship that Sunday morning, Brendan kept "hard blinking" like he was clearing his eyes to see better and was looking up and around. I asked him afterwards what he saw and he said that he saw a big, beautiful angel with big, shiny, bright wings. I held him chest-to-chest as Bonnie laid her hands on him. I asked him, "Brendan, are you ready to get healed?" and he replied, "Yes, momma." She put anointing oil on her hands, rubbed them together, laid them on both of our heads, and the last thing I heard was "Brendan." We both were slain in the Spirit with Brendan landing peacefully on my tummy. His body was like a limp noodle and he stayed that way for around ten minutes. He had never been still a day in his life, yet he remained still on top of me even after I came out of my encounter. I wasn't sure if he was just being compliant with me, but after several minutes of him not moving, I realized that the Holy Ghost had touched him. He couldn't fake that. While under the power of the Holy Ghost, which Brendan calls "Jesus loving on me," he was peaceful but moaning softly in a good way. When he came out of it, he could hardly speak and his first response was, "Jesus said a lot of words to me but I can't remember them all." He then said to me, "Momma, Jesus came to see me and so did the angels. The angels were gathering around. The girl angels have golden wings and the boy angels have silver wings. [I was moaning] because I could feel where God was healing me here" and pointed to his heart. He continued, "Jesus told me that it is okay and don't worry. That He's healing me. That He's still working on me. That He will heal me and that I will go to heaven one day." Brendan kept saying, "God healed me and God healed Mommy today." Before that moment, I don't remember Brendan ever telling me he could see angels. After that encounter, we chose to believe that we would see Brendan healed very soon. We didn't know what it would look like or even how to walk out that healing, but we chose to focus on the truth.

As a thirteen-year-old, Brendan recalls that encounter by saying, "If I were to look back on it, it would be like I saw it yesterday. In the encounter, I was standing up but then froze as I saw an angel. His presence was terrifying. I saw him and knew I wanted him to protect me. He was dressed like a knight in armor and his wings resembled metallic. Then, the rest of them showed up. There were two sections of angels standing in three rows like if they were in bleachers, but there were no bleachers. They floated there with barely even moving their wings. They had large, chrome-like swords and I was in awe and speechless. Then there were two bigger angels who had gigantic swords. I then saw something like fire, but it looked like ice. It was dark blue like a really cold fire. Then, Jesus showed up. It was terrifying and I thought I would physically die from seeing Him. He was very bright, so bright like the sun. He was ten times brighter than the brightest light, that if you looked directly into it, you would go blind. He was wearing something that looked white, but you could see through it and all I could see was the light inside of Him. His eyes were like fire just like it says in Revelation. I couldn't say anything. All I could do was listen. I thought to myself that Jesus must be so holy to have all of these angels there when He showed up. It was the clearest time I've ever heard Him. He said to me that I was going to be healed and not to worry. Then he talked about warfare and then told me to tell my mom. When I woke up, it felt like two minutes had passed, but it had been twenty. I wondered if I was blind from seeing the light and I was unable to speak for the next two or three hours."

Even after the prophetic word and powerful encounters, nothing seemed to change for Brendan for two years. I continued to declare, "No, my child is not autistic!" At every altar call, we went up front for prayer and remembered the story of Naaman. Fast-forward to the spring of 2013, and we found out that Chris Gore was coming to speak. I didn't know anything about him, but someone told me that he had seen breakthrough with children who had autism. So, I started preparing Brendan for two to three weeks before Chris arrived. On May 25th, we were driving to the meeting and I said to Brendan, "Wouldn't it be cool if he prayed and your autism was gone?" He said to me, "Mom, one of the things I like about being autistic is that I'm creative. I don't want to stop being creative." He was afraid that if he were healed, that he would lose that part of his identity. I responded, "Creativity is a gift from God. Once He gives you a gift, He never takes it back! You can be healed from autism without losing your creativity!" He replied, "Awesome! I want that guy to pray for me!" It was after the service, around 11:00pm when Brendan received prayer. It was so late, that I told Brendan to just go touch his shirt to be healed. However, Brendan held fast in faith and tenacity. He said "Momma, No! I want him to pray for me." I walked up to Chris and felt terrible because it was late and I didn't want to bother him. When Brendan asked Chris to pray for him and why, I just knew that my child's faith had shaken the heavens. Without skipping a beat, Chris smiled and it's like something turned on inside of him. He didn't tarry a long time in prayer. He just quickly prayed and then what he did next touched us so much. He asked Brendan to pray for him for more creativity. Here this man, who we consider to be a mighty man of God, is staying up late at night to pray for us, and he honored my son and us by recognizing what he saw on Brendan's life. It gave Brendan an opportunity to give back. Nothing really crazy or amazing happened in that moment, or at least nothing in the physical: no shaking, no tears, just peace. But there was so much faith it was almost tangible.

On the way home, Brendan said that he felt "it" lift off, like something came off of him. He said that it felt like it was gone and that he had been healed of autism. He felt a weight come off, like a balloon. Later, he recalled that moment by saying, "I felt something coming off me. It's like you're carrying a heavy backpack and you were carrying it for years and then you take it off and it feels really good." After that night, the signs of autism weren't completely gone, but they were immediately better. We felt like the Lord released us to wean him off of the medications and began a very quick process of doing so. He had been on medications since he was two and a half years old for both his behavior and to help him sleep. Brendan hadn't slept through the night since he was eighteen months old, and now he started sleeping through the entire night! By July 2nd of 2013, he had taken his last medications. Brendan also started engaging in the world around him. He maintained his creativity and will draw out what he is thinking. He even recently started writing stories. He's still a more introverted kid, but that's a part of his personality. The autism was just a perversion of what Brendan was actually created to be like. Things started to change after that moment of prayer, but his total healing was still a process.

During this process, all of his odd behaviors didn't stop immediately. We would make some progress and then feel like we backtracked. We would have to stand firm in his healing. I knew that any behaviors were just lying symptoms and that they had to go in Jesus' Name. We chose to believe that God is Who He says He is and that what Jesus did on the cross was enough. He's the God of "I'm going to make you a promise" and He keeps His promises.

In January of 2014, we started changing his diet and that made a big difference for us too. Sometimes there are things we have to do. It's not our acts that get us to Heaven. However, God wants us to partner with Him. It might not look the same for every family, and families have to focus on what they can, one thing at a time. We had to make choices in this process of him being fully healed. Then, one day we woke up and realized that we had a different kid! Our son had become fully connected with us! Over the course of a year, we saw all of the autistic behaviors go away! Brendan didn't lose any of his creativity and he still likes to have ideas and invent things. In regards to how it has changed his life, he stated, "The autism would make me afraid of things. I used to be afraid of some things that now I'm not afraid of anymore. I was afraid of surgeries a lot and of haircuts and I'm not anymore. The noise of the clippers scared me the most and after I was healed, I could sit through the whole thing and never flinch once!"

In January of 2015, David Wagner prophesied over him that he was going to be growing in stature and favor with God and man. Brendan has always been excessively small, so his response to the word was, "Mom, did you hear that? He says I'm going to grow!"

Brendan has always been at least four or five inches shorter than his younger brother and he is now the same height! His growth chart looks incredible! From May of 2013 to the present, his weight increased from being in the 10th percentile to the 25th percentile and his height jumped from being in the 5th percentile to now the 30th percentile! Considering he spent the majority of his life below the 10th percentile, this is a huge growth for him and it all began with those first seeds of healing and hope planted in 2011. Thank you Jesus!

Here's a more recent statement from one of Brendan's doctors:

13. GENERAL COMMENTS *(Include Functional Levels)*

Has not been seen or treated for ADHD or autism @ this office since 2011.

If you are in a place of losing hope, of being on the edge of giving up: don't! After hundreds of prayers and thousands of tears, the seed sprouted for us and became a flower! I declare and release breakthrough over you in Jesus' Name! If He would do it for my Brendan, He will do it for you! Begin to celebrate the small stuff. I bless you with an outrageous amount of courage to put your stake in the ground, to choose to believe the Truth instead of the facts, and to set your face like flint on Jesus, because He is the source of all strength and comfort.

He's the God of "I'm going to make you a promise" and He keeps His promises.

A KEY FOR BREAKTHROUGH

CHRIS GORE

It's been a pleasure to know Brendan and his family over the years and to see how he is growing up into a young man. His story emphasizes what was talked about in the introduction and is key in our children walking in divine health. No matter what our circumstances, we cannot let the conditions we face become part of our identity. Often we hear from people that autism, cerebral palsy, and other conditions are a part of someone's identity. We get asked why would we ever want these children healed and to lose their extreme creativity or ability to love. Brendan's story perfectly illustrates the heart of the Father and challenges us to believe that God is big enough to help our children maintain their sense of love, humor, and personality while taking away the symptoms of anxiety, chaos, isolation, and the like. Brendan is fully his creative and musical self, just now without the challenges that autism brought to his life.

Brendan's story also speaks to us about the importance of not taking offense with God when it seems like He hasn't moved on our behalf after hundreds of prayers.   Brendan's family had taken him for prayer so many times, both in faith and in what they called "humiliation" with seemingly no results. It could've been so easy for them to become offended at God and simply resolve that God no longer wanted to heal their son. What would've happened if they gave up right before the moment he had his encounter with Jesus? What if they had allowed disappointment, hopelessness, fear, and offense stop them from receiving prayer just one more time?

We went on a similar journey in 2008 when our daughter Charlotte had to undergo a spinal fusion from the top of her neck to the base of her spine. It was a pretty traumatic operation. She lost a massive amount of blood, her eyes were swollen shut for ten days, and she was in such incredible pain. It was so difficult as a father to see her hurting and not be able to take it away. There was a defining moment for me in the intensive care ward in which I shut the door and blinds and began to play worship. I pulled out an empty chair and said, "That's for you, devil. Sit there and watch what's about to happen." I began to pour out my heart in worship to God like never before. I wasn't worshipping God in order to coerce Him to do something, but simply in adoration for Who He is. There had been some offenses toward Him in my heart and we needed to have a frank conversation. An agreement with God was made that day at her bedside. I said to God, "Whether she makes it through all of this or not, regardless of the outcome, I will never be offended at You for the things that haven't happened.

We see in Matthew 14 that Jesus also had every reason to be upset and disappointed. He had just received news that his dear friend, John the Baptist, had been beheaded. It says that Jesus went up on the mountainside by Himself to pray. I propose that Jesus went to be alone so that He could be refreshed and reminded of the goodness, faithfulness, and love of His heavenly Father in the midst of His pain. We need to do the same. What we do with the discouragements of today will determine the fruitfulness of what we will walk in tomorrow. What would it look like if we actually aligned ourselves to the truth that the absence of a miracle doesn't define the nature or the goodness of our Father? No matter what we see or don't see, He is a good God. Yes, we live in mystery and tension, but we need to make sure that even then, offenses are not being built. One of the greatest ways we can determine if we have an offense with God is in if we can't celebrate in someone else's breakthrough, especially when their victory is exactly what we need. When we can truly rejoice with others, we actually position ourselves to receive that same breakthrough. So, let's rejoice with what Jesus has done in Brendan's life and be a people who know how to celebrate!

REFLECTION #1

Before you read on, take a moment to be honest with the Father. Whether you are in a really great place in life or stuck in disappointments, He wants to hear your heart. True connection and freedom with God is on the other side of vulnerability. He will meet you in it, but will never leave you there.

REFLECTION #2

Our identities and destinies are found in Jesus and not the circumstances or conditions in our lives. Take time to ask Holy Spirit to show you the true identity of your son or daughter and even yourself and write it down. Place this somewhere where you will frequently see it and be reminded of God's perspective and promises.

CHAPTER 2

IN AN INSTANT

PETER & LILY'S STORY

For the longest time, I was in denial that anything was different with my little Lily. However, when she was around two years old, she began doing incredibly dangerous things that we couldn't deny. If I took my eyes off of her for even a second, she would be climbing the fence, trying to climb up on the roof, going into the neighbor's yard, running to the next aisle in a store, etc. I seriously don't know how I ever shopped at all. There were many times I had to restrain her and carry her out of stores kicking and screaming. As all eyes were on us in those moments, I imagine people thought I was a bad parent, but there was really nothing else I could do. It was scary because she couldn't recognize temperatures or pain either, so it was difficult to know when she was hurt or feeling sick. She wasn't talking to me and would throw fits about everything. It was a battle to get her into and out of the house and the car, so going anywhere was a real struggle. At times, she was also violent and would spontaneously come up behind me and hit me over the head with things. She scratched all of the kids at her preschool so much so that she was eventually kicked out. Around the age of three she was diagnosed with severe autism and we thought that she might have to be institutionalized. Our life was in chaos.

A couple of years after Lily was born, I was pregnant again, but this time with a son. I was looking forward to having a chance to experience the things I missed during Lily's early years due to the autism. Peter was a really sweet baby. He would coo and babble at us and was everything we had hoped for. Then the unimaginable happened when suddenly at eighteen months of age, he became quiet. The affectionate noises stopped. In my mind, there was no way that he could also be diagnosed with autism. I remember crying on the floor for hours when that thought actually became our reality. "How could this be happening again?!" In that moment of grief, God's presence came in the room and He said to me, "I'm going to heal him." I was on cloud nine for the first few days as I was anticipating that at any instant, Peter would be healed and talk. This journey of waiting for the healing to manifest became a training ground for me of what it looks like to hold on to a promise. All I knew to do was to hold on. To keep me from being in a continuous state of pain and grief, I devoted myself to serving other people. When you see God working in other people's lives, you have assurance for yourself too. It's as if seeing God's heart for others helps you to realize that His heart is for you too. Despite my prayers and believing that Peter would be instantly healed, he continued to withdraw and regressed even more.

As I look back, there was a moment when life and circumstances became really awful. I cried out to God, "If You don't do something, I am going to die!" It was physically and emotionally draining in every way. I needed to do something to save myself for the sake of my kids. I was lying in bed and listening to a podcast. As soon as the minister said "fire," my body rocked back and forth and I felt electricity pulsating through me. After that, I had more awareness of the spiritual realm. I would experience realms of the spirit where I was convinced of the truth of God. In rough times, I thought to myself that if I could just get back into that realm, that I could be rescued. I continued to fast, pray, and stand on His word and began asking the Lord for confirmation that we were going to be okay. I asked Lily's teacher what it would look like for her to progress. Her response was that she needed to cooperate. So, I took that specific thing to the Lord and warred in the spirit on behalf of my daughter. A month later, we still hadn't seen breakthrough and I was feeling super discouraged. I cried out to God that I needed a sign and the very next day, to my joy and surprise, Lily received an award at school for cooperation! God was reassuring me loud and clear!

When my daughter was seven and my son was four, we decided to go to Bethel Church to pursue healing for them. We were desperate! The experience that my family had at the Healing Rooms was so incredible! The healing team prayed for Lily and Peter, but also prayed for me and my other daughter as well. I received two prophetic words that completely wrecked me in a good way and left me sobbing in one of the rooms. When the team started praying, they began by rebuking autism. I was such a wreck that all I can remember is that I got on my knees to pray and was being transformed. In that moment, I was being freed from previous mindsets and started seeing things differently. It was something that I knew needed to happen, but I couldn't have done myself.

When they began praying for Peter and Lily, I noticed that both of my kids were letting the team pray for them and touch them, which isn't a normal reaction for them to have. However, what touched my heart the most was the way they loved my children. They saw my kids and their hearts and their strengths, not their current disabilities. It was the best day ever for us and immediately my oldest daughter stated with confidence, "They are healed!"

The next day, we brought Peter and Lily to Bethel's Sunday school class for children with special needs called "Breakthrough." Lily had said a few words to one of the teachers and had interacted with her with a plastic bowling ball set. She thought this was normal for Lily, but we were so surprised! She would never have connected on this level with someone who was a stranger! I also noticed, like at the Healing Rooms, how much more at peace they were. I received a prophetic word from the team and we left encouraged.

We noticed immediately that there was a shift with both Lily and Peter. There was so much peace! They were more content and began talking more! Everyone noticed it. Previously, they had been irritable a lot. Everything would rub them the wrong way. They would be impatient, transitioning was always difficult, and there was not much joy or peace in the house. They would become frustrated when things wouldn't happen as they had planned or if there was a break in their routines. A lot of these struggles have gone away and they have been more peaceful, relaxed, and content. Joy and happiness have been restored in our house!

I also had them both on a very restrictive diet. If they ate certain things, they would be awake all night in a rage and would have skin and bowel issues. I altogether stopped taking them to places that had food. They would see food that they couldn't have, steal it, and then I was left with violent, irritable, and angry children the rest of the day. Although they are not 100% healed in this area, so much healing happened that they can now eat the typical diet of other American kids like chicken nuggets and french fries. That change alone has made life so much easier!

Joy and happiness have been restored in our house!

I believed that noticeable breakthrough had taken place, but wanted a third party to acknowledge it too. I knew going back to school would be the true test. I took them to school the first week and the teacher's words were, "I am shocked!" Previously, my daughter Lily would have a lot of behavioral problems in school and would often run away. She would have difficulty transitioning and was not talking as much as what we knew she could. My main concern was that she might have had a mood disorder. Again, the teacher was shocked when she returned to school! Her attitude had changed, she was happier, she had no transition problems, she was talking more, and had no issues running away. Before, we would need staff on hand to help us even get her out of the car at school. That improved by 90%! She also used to get so angry and would kick and attack my face when I would try to brush her hair. This was so significant that brushing her hair without these reactions was actually a written goal in her IEP (Individualized Education Program). After receiving ministry that weekend, she would allow me to brush it and her IEP now reports that she comes to school with bows in her hair! The staff now has to make new goals for Lily because she has met all of them! There are times when we all look at her and say to ourselves, "Who is this kid?"

We also saw immediate changes in Peter. Even though he was in a special needs class, I would get calls from his school to pick him up early. After prayer, he became much more regulated and could remain in the classroom for the entire day! His teacher would comment to us about his "awesome" days! He started talking a lot more, using two-word phrases from time to time, and began singing parts of songs in school, and he hadn't done any of that before. What people may not understand by reading this is that my son was pretty much non-verbal before this! It was hard to get him to even make a sound. He is also much more obedient now too. At times, he used to run away into the middle of the street and not listen when we told him to come back. It was scary and dangerous. Now, he is much better and is paying attention and obeying! Also, Peter recently had his 5th birthday party and was actually interested in his presents. Before, he would open them, throw them to the side, and wouldn't even take the toys out of the box. This was the first birthday where he was actually interested in the toys and waited patiently while his other sister opened all of the boxes for him. What a happy birthday for us all!

Although we are still believing God for more healing, what I've seen in our journey is that the healing would come in chunks. There was a lot of peace right away, but then some warfare would come and try to take the ground that we had gained. I would just continue to fast, pray, and declare the Word. I was continually preparing myself to be victorious. I think for a lot of parents in a similar situation, they don't have hope or faith in their child being healed because all they can see are the behaviors in front of them. We've been conditioned to think that since we've lived a certain way for so long, that that will always be our permanent reality. In an instant, our reality changed!

In an instant, our reality changed!

A KEY FOR BREAKTHROUGH

CHRIS GORE

In hearing Peter and Lily's mom tell their story, it became evident that she had found a significant key in the process of seeing breakthrough in our children. She knew how to celebrate and notice every breakthrough, whether it seemed big or small. From her children simply allowing someone to touch their shoulder to assessments changing on IEPs, it was all significant to this family. Every miracle is spectacular because they are all impossible without Jesus!

Learn how to celebrate in every breakthrough and stay in the place of being in the awe of God. As parents and caregivers of children with special needs, we can have a lot of negative situations come at us and it can become very easy to go to a place of discouragement and hopelessness. However, when we can keep our eyes on what has happened and what is happening, versus focusing on what hasn't happened yet, we can find ourselves living in a place of encouragement. With our daughter, we get excited when she makes a new sound, sleeps well, or feeds herself a potato chip. All of these moments are significant to us.

The more we can stay connected to Jesus as our source, and focus on what has happened and what is happening, the more we're encouraged and begin accessing the power and blessing of thankfulness. The manifestations of the kingdom increase as we learn to give thanks. The more we give thanks, the more we see. In John 6, we see a multitude of hungry people who need a miraculous intervention and then we see a young lad with five barley loaves and two fish. He didn't have enough to feed the entire 5,000 men, that is, not until after Jesus gave thanks for it. If God is outside of time, which He is, should we not be celebrating our breakthroughs before they even happen because we know that the price was already paid for at the cross?

At the same time that we are thankful, we also stay hungry for more breakthrough. There is wisdom in the tension we carry between thanksgiving and hunger. If we are always thankful without hunger for more breakthrough, it can lead to plateauing at a place of contentment. However, if we are always hungry without thankfulness, it can lead to desperation, which can lead to unbelief, which can then lead to unfruitfulness. As you celebrate in the big and small breakthroughs, remember to pray for the more as well.

So, what would it look like if we began feasting on what we have seen instead of feeding on the discouragement that can come from focusing on what we haven't seen yet? What would it look like if we just became the most thankful people and began to celebrate life, every little breakthrough, and healing even before we see it?

REFLECTION #3

There is power in remembering what the Lord has done. Begin a gratitude journal or list of all of the things that you have seen positively change in your son or daughter's life. Continue to write down every breakthrough, big or small, and celebrate in what Jesus is doing! Share it with people who will put the fuel of faith on your fire of hope.

CHAPTER 3

GRIPPED BY FAITH

SAMUEL'S STORY

My husband and I clearly felt that the Lord had put it on our hearts to have a son and name him Samuel. We were so delighted when he was born, but from day two of his life, I could see he could not handle physical contact. Latching on for nursing was enraging for him. We got through fourteen months of nursing, but it was no small task. Every diaper change, clothes change, etc. would erupt him into extreme, red-faced, screaming.

He was very delayed in crawling, walking, and then speech. At two and a half years old, the word "autism" first crossed my ears; bringing with it a completely broken, devastated heart for me. We knew he had a big call on his life, but this diagnosis felt larger than life and that hope for his calling died. I ended up with adrenal issues and felt like I was just surviving for a season.

He was officially diagnosed at three years old and our journey down this road continued. When we would go to church, I'd have to keep him occupied or he would be inattentive, not be able to sit still, and would roll all over the floor making strange noises. He was all over the place, like a very unfocused spiral. While in kindergarten, I never knew what his day looked like because he couldn't communicate to me at all what had transpired. It was like once a month, he would give me one sentence. Throughout the first grade, if something were upsetting to him, he would behaviorally act out instead of being able to verbally process things. There were times when he had been upset for weeks and we wouldn't know it or know why because he couldn't get the words out to tell us. He had his own type of language. Baths and showers continued to be overwhelming and traumatic for him at this age as well.

Three years in, the Lord gave me a real wake-up call: I got out of my devastation, got on my face, and cried out from the depths of my being. This crying out lasted five years. I have a distinct memory from the beginning of this season of looking at Sam and from the very core of my person rose up the words "You're going to be okay! It's going to be okay!" He had a brief moment of clarity and actually looked me right in the eye and said "Okay." I could see I connected in that moment with the eternal Sam not the autistic Sam. I saw relief and confidence in his eyes, and for a flicker of a moment we had connection. From that second on, a Holy fire rose up in me to see Samuel released from this prison and to walk out his call in complete freedom bought and paid for by his Savior Jesus Christ. Over this time, we saw a continual progress in Sam emerging into his freedom.

There were some other benchmarks where I noticed a shift. When he was six years old, our church had a guest speaker who prayed for Sam and within a month, I saw a progression of him becoming more and more clear. He was able to be present more and hear what I was saying. Before, it was like he would just be in constant motion and wouldn't know what was going on. It was enough of a progression that I could see a difference, but wasn't complete clarity yet. However, he was making a step in the right direction!

During these five years of pressing in, we made some big changes and took some risks. In September of 2015, we took Sam out of public school where he had IEPs and a full-time aide and put him into a Christian private school. It was a scary move because we were leaving behind all of his support, but we knew the Lord was prompting us so we said yes. In public school, he would have a person with him all day and now I was bringing him to a place where he had no extra person and would have to do what everyone else was doing. We were shocked to see what happened. He went from just reaching the academic benchmark to straight As, from hating school to loving it, and from very bad behavior to getting "outstanding" every day on his report! He also went from full-time help to needing no extra help, no aide, and no IEP! A holy atmosphere around him made such a difference. We also felt that the Lord would have us go organic in foods and other household products. This also brought health as we embraced what life was meant to look like in the Garden from the beginning.

Sam is now a very happy, easy-going, ten-year-old boy who is best friends with his nine-year-old brother. He's very good at giving eye contact and having conversations with whomever about whatever. We have really deep conversations together and he can even recall and reflect on what things were like before and how different he is now. He's very aware and conscientious. He´s always been compassionate but is way more now and loves to give hugs. He also continues to have a fantastic imagination and is artistic like his dad and will sketch for hours. He's totally thriving, so much happier, and loves the Lord.

During all of this, we never embraced autism as a part of Sam's identity. We used the diagnoses to get the services he needed, but beyond that, we treated him as typical and called him up beyond any limitations. Of course, this was balanced in giving him grace and the space he needed. It was like a fine-tuned juggling act. When he questioned differences with himself and others, I explained that we are all unique and have things to overcome and positive things to embrace. I would tell him nightly "Remember, God named you Samuel" and pray thanking God for complete rightness in our brains and bodies and all that Jesus paid for.

For five years, we stood before the Throne of Grace, agreeing with the intercession of Christ and in return received a letter stating Sam's un-diagnosis! There are still a few little lingering things that he needs breakthrough in, like chewing on his shirt when he's nervous, but according to the doctor, he no longer has enough symptoms to be autistic!

Here is a screenshot of one of the statements from Sam's report:

He is no longer disabled as of 10/2017.

God is faithful to His word! Sometimes just standing firm in faith and in His promise of power is winning. God is very kind and gives everything we need to make sure we overcome in the battle.

To other parents who are waiting for healing, I would encourage you to appreciate and really be thankful for every milestone because the truth is that even "small" breakthroughs are really big to our families. They have the power to bring all of the hope, encouragement, faith, and strength that we need. I would also recommend journaling every positive thing that happens as a testimonial to the Lord. It's so good to record all those milestones so you can look back in remembrance like the Israelites did when they set up the memorial stones. Even if it is something that may not be significant to anyone else, you know that the Lord did something in that moment. During days that aren't so bright, when maybe you don't see progression or even regression, you can look back at what's already happened and keep your faith. It is so life-giving to do. Remember, just as the Lord gave us a promise concerning our son Samuel, He has a redeeming plan that is so much greater than what we see. Partner with His plan and grab hold of it for your family!

A KEY FOR BREAKTHROUGH

CHRIS GORE

Samuel's mom was gripped by faith in the promises that God had spoken over her son before he was even born. On my journey in healing ministry, the topic of faith often arises from the hearts of praying people seeking to know if they have enough faith for a miracle. If they have accepted Jesus Christ as their Lord and Savior, the answer is always "Yes." Romans 12:3 states that, " . . . God has dealt to each one a measure of faith." That's great news! This means that on your best faith-filled day or on your worst, hopeless day, that faith still exists inside of you. Faith is not a feeling that we muster up inside, but it is an awareness of the Faithful One who took residence inside of us.

Hebrews 12:2 reads, "Looking unto Jesus, the author and finisher of *our* faith; who for the joy that was set before Him endured the cross, despising the shame, and has sat down at the right hand of the throne of God." Many scholars believe that the words "of our" should actually read "of" so instead that passage would say, "Looking unto Jesus, the author and finisher *of* faith . . ." We have a part in co-laboring with Heaven, but faith isn't about us, it's about Jesus. In this testimony, Samuel's mom did what she felt in her heart by setting aside time to pray specifically about their situation, but it wasn't the faith *of* a mom that sustained her for five years, it was her fixing her eyes on the faith of Christ.

Many families wonder what they need to do to get more faith to see breakthrough for their children and want to know the answer to having great faith. The answer to having great faith is actually simple . . . stop worrying about your faith. Don't get me wrong, faith is the currency of Heaven and without faith, it is impossible to please God (Hebrews 11:6). However, we don't experience more faith by focusing on our own faith, but rather by anchoring it to the faith of Christ. His faith is never wavering. As we look to Jesus, our faith then is not found in our own prayers or feelings, but rather in the nature of a Person. The faith that He authored that is living inside of us arises as we simply hang out with Him.

As you are focusing on the faith of Christ, you can also do things in the natural to partner with the atmosphere of faith. As you see progress happen with your child, it is important to know who the people are in your life that will join you in celebrating. Look for people who will champion your family and agree with the promises and prophetic words that have been spoken over your child's life. We weren't meant to do this alone.

REFLECTION #4

Matthew 17:20 states, "Truly I tell you, if you have faith as small as a mustard seed, you can say to this mountain, 'Move from here to there,' and it will move. Nothing will be impossible for you." As a reminder of this promise, we encourage you to take an actual mustard seed and tape it either beside this scripture or any other place that Holy Spirit highlights to you. Be reminded when you look at it that nothing is impossible!

REFLECTION #5

Children often have faith in that whatever their parents tell them is the truth. They don't "try" to believe it, they just "do" because they know the heart of their parents. Take a moment to access childlikeness and see any difficult situation through the lens of a child who is looking up to a faith-filled Father. What does He show you?

CHAPTER 4

TAUGHT BY JESUS

VIO'S STORY

My husband had a powerful dream around the time that we realized that our son Vio was different than other children. In the dream, we were on a cruise ship and we had a bomb in our cabin. We knew that when this bomb blew up, the ship would go down, everyone would die, and it would be our fault. The bomb was ticking and my husband went to open it. We were expecting it to explode at any second when he saw it and said "Oops." It wasn't a bomb, but rather was a box wrapped in gift paper. Inside the box was a beautiful, ticking, golden clock. What seemed to be something lethal, deadly, and destroying was a gift instead. We knew at once the dream was about Vio. At the time, we had been living with this "bomb" feeling. If I can be honest, taking care of Vio was draining to our lives and to our marriage. It felt like every aspect of our life was like a bomb, ready to explode any minute and needing to be cared for with extreme caution. After that dream, we realized that Vio was our beautiful gift. He was our little golden clock. He was very delayed in crawling, walking, and then speech. At two and a half years old, the word "autism" first crossed my ears; bringing with it a completely broken, devastated heart for me. We knew he had a big call on his life, but this diagnosis felt larger than life and that hope for his calling died. I ended up with adrenal issues and felt like I was just surviving for a season.

Vio is our oldest son and has had significant breakthrough in autism. During the first three months of his life, everything seemed alright, but then I realized that something was different. He wouldn't make eye contact or laugh and his body tension was floppy. Within the first year, it became crystal clear that something was definitely not going right. Then, the screaming began. He would scream, scream, scream for any and all reasons. He was hard to console and it was difficult to go anywhere with him. I have thankfully overcome this now, but at the time, I had so much shame regarding Vio. I couldn't go with other mommies to things, like toddler play dates, because I was so ashamed as Vio was very different. When he started walking, I tried to take him to the park with the other mommies. Their kids would be playing together in the sandbox or on the playground, but not my Vio. He would run and vanish and I was always left chasing after him. I never got to connect with the other moms because of this and started to live a very isolated lifestyle. The shame attached to our situation made the idea of going out worse than the thought of just staying home. We both lived in a bubble during that time of his life. It was horrible! I remember one especially painful memory during this time. It was summer and while I was stuck inside with Vio, I could hear outside that everyone was playing, laughing, and having fun. Not only were we inside, we also had to have the blinds shut as Vio was sensitive to the sun. It was one of my darkest moments. It was hell. I was a Christian and cried out to God, "Lord, my life is over. What do you want me to do now?"

One of our first glimmers of breakthrough happened in the winter of 2010/2011. My husband is a university professor and he had a scholarship for Toronto University. He proposed for all of us to go for a semester. I thought to myself, "How can we do this with an eleven-month-old and an autistic boy? How can we travel in the winter? It's absurd!" It was January 1st of 2011 and I told the Lord my specific request. I was going to open one of the many books that were next to my bed and that He would have to show me in this exact book that I have to go to Toronto. I told Him that "It has to be crystal clear, or I won't go." I took a book at random out of my pile, flipped it open, and saw that one of the chapter headings read, "Toronto is the answer." I was so depressed at the time that I didn't get excited and thought, "This is too obvious. It must be the devil." We continued on to Toronto, but I still said to the Lord, "I need a second proof." I went to a healing room with Vio and we received prayer. That morning, in their healing rooms, there were three other autistic children who received prayer. This was not a common thing there, so I knew that God was confirming again to me that we needed to be in Toronto. I thought to myself, "Lord, You announced it with a book and then with this. Today, there must be a healing with Vio." However, nothing apparently changed when they prayed for him. We were about to take a bus back to where we were staying when a lady asked if we wanted to go to their soaking room. We had never experienced one before and knowing my Vio, he wouldn't last long at all in a room like that. I could imagine him running around and being a distraction while other people would be trying to focus on God. Despite this, she convinced us to give it a try and there we saw the first signs of breakthrough! In our daily life, Vio would never stay in the same place longer than five minutes, and we found ourselves staying there on the sofa for three and a half hours! Vio could barely talk at the time and there he said to me, "Mama, can you read me something from the Bible?" I whispered the book of Psalms in his ear the entire time. Toronto was a significant part of our story and God was so gracious to confirm it to me twice!

Around that time, Vio began to see Jesus and angels and he continues to have regular encounters with the angelic to this day. I will always remember the Sunday when we were at our church and my husband decided to stay on the empty balcony level with Vio during the service. All of a sudden, Vio started pointing and whispering excitedly, "Papa, Daddy, Daddy, do you see that?! Jesus is there!" This was very unusual as at that time, he wouldn't address his father directly, neither did he point to things. A guy was playing worship, so my husband asked if that's what he was pointing to. Vio emphatically said, "No. Not him!" and pointed to a corner where there was nobody. It was very interesting, so my husband asked Vio what Jesus looked like. Without hesitation, Vio replied, "He is dressed in bright, long clothes. His hair is dark and there is hair on his face [a beard]." A few days later, Vio stated to his dad, "Daddy, Jesus talked to me on Sunday. He said, 'Vio, you are smart. You are precious.'" Then he said that Jesus told him, "Vio, follow the wind." Imagine, he was four years old and could hardly talk or put two words together and he said these things. He had never used the words "smart," "precious," or "wind" before because his language was somewhat impaired during that time and very limited. To us, the word "wind" represented Holy Spirit and God's presence and direction in Vio's life.

Another angelic encounter happened when I was home alone with the kids. I was tossing and turning in bed one night. There were so many things that I was worried about that kept racing through my mind and I could not sleep. Vio was lying in bed next to me and I was sure he was asleep, when all of a sudden he asked me, "Mama, why are you worried? My angel told me that you are worried. You don't need to be worried. Everything is all right." Wow! He's so in touch with the spiritual dimension in everyday life. When Vio talks about angels, it is a beautiful thing. He says that his two angels even have names. However, what is even more important is that the angels always point back to Jesus. It's so crystal clear it's about Jesus and the angels do not let themselves be misused or exalted above Him in any way. I have been touched so much by how my Vio interacts with the spirit realm!

We continued to see a certain amount of improvement with Vio, but noticed that he still could not relate with other people or have empathy. He just didn't connect with things that were happening. I felt so much pain in my heart as I saw his little brother so desperately wanting him as a playmate. They were both being robbed of this sibling bond and us as a whole family. Little did I know that all of that was about to change.

My sister-in-law got a book by a guy named Chris Gore and encouraged me to read it because it had a chapter in there about a girl named Hope who was healed. So I got the book, read it, and was electrified when I read about Hope. I thought to myself, "I need to get in touch with this guy." I began checking on his speaking itinerary and found out that he was coming that year only hours from where we lived in Germany. We had to go there and began making plans!

Two nights before we went to the healing rooms that Chris was leading, I was walking Vio to school and he said, "Mama, I had a dream last night. It was a very strange dream. Jesus came to me and He said to me, 'Eat bread and drink wine and I will give you life.' I was allowed to drink wine Mama. I'm just a kid and can't drink wine, but tonight I've been drinking wine." I was surprised and fascinated, so asked him, "What did you do?" He said, "Then I had bread. Very, very, yummy bread." Jesus had visited my son and taught him communion! Later, we found out that the revelation of communion was very important to Chris as well.

> *Jesus came to me and He said to me, 'Eat bread and drink wine and I will give you life.'*

The night before the healing rooms, I told my son that we were going to go see a specialist in the morning, but did not tell him that the specialist actually meant going to the healing rooms. As we were driving to the church, Vio told me that he had another dream. Here's how he described it to me, "Mama, I had another dream last night. I was in a pit. I was there and had no chance to get out. Then, Jesus and his friend came and told me that they were there to set me free and that I would never have to go back. He pulled me out of the pit and I was free." We decided that when we arrived, we should look for this friend of Jesus.

We came to the healing rooms and were so immensely blessed by the love of the Bethel team and the local staff of the church that day! The moment we entered the building, Vio exclaimed, "Ahh, a lot of angels are here!" Vio had one of the best days of his life there. He had so much joy seeing Jesus and the angels do all these great things for him and for others. One of Chris' team members met us and shared her heart for children with disabilities. Just in that moment, I could feel my son's spirit was opening up. She asked if they could pray for me first, which was a surprise as I was there solely for Vio. As they prayed, I began crying and as I began crying, my son looked up at me and said in German, "You are crying. You are being moved, Mama" to which the tears began to fall even more. Right there in front of my eyes, Vio was beginning to identify my emotions, which he had never done before! Something had changed right in the moment they prayed for me, and they hadn't even prayed for Vio yet! They prayed for me some more and he expressed wanting to dance, which again was another new thing for him. So, we talked as we watched Vio freely dancing away on the church's platform stage! They knew that we had to begin our three-hour drive home and wouldn't be able to make it to the evening service, so arranged with Chris to pray for Vio before we left. The moment Chris entered, Vio shouted, "That's the guy! That's the guy from the dream! He's the friend of Jesus!" Chris prayed for him and there was nothing spectacular about it. It wasn't a show. Vio allowed Chris to simply hold him in his arms and he was rocking him very gently like a daddy. All of a sudden, Vio started dancing on the platform even more saying, "I'm so happy! Joy is coming into my head!" He then offered me coffee, which he had never done before. For me as a mother, this was a beautiful moment. He was recognizing my needs and how to make me happy. He poured some coffee and then poured a lot of sugar in it. It probably had more sugar in it than coffee. It was the best worst coffee I ever had! I was so happy!

We began our three-hour drive home when Vio suddenly asked me in German, "Mama, was bedeutet Empathie?" which in English is "What is empathy?" He over-pronounced the word like you do when you read and spell a foreign word for the first time. "Empathy" is a very unusual word for even adults to use in German with only maybe half of them even knowing that word. There is a different word we would use instead, but Vio clearly asked about "empathy." I explained to him that empathy meant the capacity to understand the feelings of others and to feel with them. I then asked him where he had heard that word. He replied to me, "Jesus just whispered in my ear that I am going to learn empathy now, so I wanna know what it is I am supposed to learn." Wow! This word and understanding the feelings of another person is a feature that an autistic child could hardly have, so I knew it was God. We then invented a funny song that was a proclamation of an empathetic Vio. Vio was shouting the word "empathie" and I could sense the spiritual effect it had in the atmosphere when he spoke it. We had great fun in the car! We turned on the radio and as soon as we did, the DJ said that listeners were to wish for songs but only such starting with the letter "V". Vio was convinced that this was all for him: "V" like "Vio." We continued our song game, paraphrasing all the "V" songs with new lines giving the glory to Jesus over Vio's healing and over every sickness. It was powerful!

> *He replied to me, "Jesus just whispered in my ear that I am going to learn empathy now, so I wanna know what it is I am supposed to learn."*

The days that followed were mixed. We saw some really new traits in Vio, but sometimes we had the impression that something wanted to pull him back into the pit. We kept proclaiming his healing every night. After Vio had the dream where Jesus taught and gave him communion, he began creating communion moments where we gave him bread and grape juice and he would proclaim the new life Jesus had earned for him on the cross. It was absolutely striking how he would take the initiative with this in the most unusual and fun ways. We now have the Lord's supper at any place we can imagine. He wants to take it at IKEA, McDonalds, anywhere! Even as I share this story, just today we had the Lord's supper in a Turkish Kebab shop when Vio said, "Oh, let us take the Lord's supper" with kebab bread and lemonade in his hands. He leads it and takes it very seriously. It is holy, profound, funny, and beautiful all at the same time! He continues to have revelations about it as well. He will say to me that when Jesus handed him the wine and the bread, He kept saying, "Vio du sollst leben!" which in English means, "Vio you shall live!" The Lord's supper is about restoring life as it was planned in Heaven for each individual before the beginning of time. I learned that from Vio.

Since the meeting in Germany, the most significant breakthroughs have happened with empathy, social interactions, and spiritual encounters. He is also aware of having been more autistic. In Vio's words, "When I was there [autistic], it was like I didn't get anything. It was like a veil was over my head." A lot of our friends can also see the new sweetness of his spirit. He has become so sensitive to feelings and Jesus taught him empathy just like He said He would that day in the car! Vio can now read people's emotions. He will ask me how I'm feeling and even today asked me, "Mama, are you sad? You seem sad. Is something wrong with you?" He used to not even interact with his brother and now he will try to cheer him up when he's sad and protect him when he's scared. It is both a miracle that he can recognize the emotions of sad and scared as well as the fact that he is interacting with his brother in this way! These massive improvements in the field of interactive play and social skills have changed their relationship and his relationships with others. He now connects and wrestles with his brother and cousins like a normal boy. He is also finally starting to have play dates which we had hoped for many years would happen. It's so beautiful!

Vio doesn't get over-stimulated like before either and is attentive instead of distracted. One time, he was talking to his dad on the phone. His dad asked, "What are you doing right now?" and Vio replied, "Oh, I am listening to music." His dad asked what kind of music to which Vio responded, "It's Holy Ghost music." It's truly amazing that he is able to have a focused conversation on the phone while some other stimulus, like music, is present. Spiritually, it is also remarkable that he is able to tell what is spiritual music and what is secular music without understanding the words of the song since the music was in English!

As a mother, I have experienced breakthroughs as well. Like I mentioned before, shame used to be my covering. Recently, I was writing with a friend who I hadn't been in touch with for twelve years. We both have PhDs and used to work really closely together on our research. Since the last time we collaborated, she became an esteemed professor and I have become a stay-at-home mommy for Vio and my two other kids. When she asked what I had been doing, I wrote her that I had been caring for my autistic son. Now for someone who had an academic career and a certain reputation, writing that might sound like a waste and devastated life. I didn't want her to feel sorry that I had to take care of a handicapped child for ten years and that's why we didn't have any academic interaction. However, when I wrote it, I thought instead to myself, "What a privilege that I have not written five books and have just cared for Vio. I had the privilege to be next to such a beautiful person such as my Vio and to grow with him. It was the best thing that has ever happened to me. I wouldn't have grown spiritually in that kind of way if it hadn't been for Vio." Shame is no longer a part of my life!

The intensity of Vio's encounters and revelations of Scripture have continued to increase. He is doing great in his spirit. He is full of revelation from God and knows exactly who he is in Jesus. I am in awe of the level of his revelation. He keeps telling the story how Jesus and His friend pulled him out of a pit and he knows that it was the pit of autism. He keeps being lifted up to Heaven and having experiences with Jesus. Last time, he was with Jesus riding a heavenly roller coaster. Things I know in my head and have not fully conquered in my heart are now so amazingly clear to Vio. After his time at the healing rooms, he would keep waking up giggling and saying. "I am rich. I am complete, you know, Mama and I am so precious." I kept asking him how he knew this and he would say, "Jesus has told me all that tonight."

Some of his encounters take us by surprise; well, most of them do. For example, my husband and I were listening to a teaching in the car about a man that had a vision of a spiritual garden that everyone has in Heaven. Vio wasn't even in the car at the time and that night, he came to our bed and said "Mama, I had a dream. You know what? I have a garden!" How could he know about the garden? He continued, "My garden has a well and the water in the well was bitter, and then Jesus walked in and threw something in the well and now it's sweet." He had no idea of that story in the Bible where Moses struck the bitter waters with a piece of wood and it turned sweet. Vio kept talking about his garden. He talked about the walls in the garden and how some of them were torn down. I saw this as Jesus healing my son's soul by taking him to the garden. Then, not long ago, he came out of the bathroom saying: "Kummer, Kummer, Kummer" which is not a typical word you would expect a child his age to say. This means "grief" in English. I asked him, "Why are you saying that word?" He responded, "This is what the devil keeps telling me to try to make me feel bad and sad." I responded, "Okay, but what are you replying?" He said, "Get lost in the Name of Jesus! And then he disappears at once!" He responded so perfectly! Sometimes I think as grown-ups we begin feeling depressed and we tend to

think that we have every reason to feel sad without realizing that it was the devil who whispered in our ears: grief, grief, grief in the first place.

God continues to teach my son other scriptures in extraordinary ways. One day, he said to me, "Mama, I need to get baptized. When I go under the water, there will be fire under the water. Jesus told me. Then, when I get up, I will be restored." How did he know about the baptism of water and fire? He was baptized Easter of 2016 and it was beautiful for the whole community to see! He is spiritually shifting atmospheres in his classroom at school too. One teacher commented that her teachings have had a greater impact since Vio has been her student. With his knowledge of Biblical truths, he speaks out openly in her lessons and gets to the core of things. His teachers have been deeply touched.

> *Sometimes I think as grown-ups we begin feeling depressed and we tend to think that we have every reason to feel sad without realizing that it was the devil who whispered in our ears: grief, grief, grief in the first place.*

So much healing has happened with Vio, but there's still more that we are believing for. There are days that are still extremely hard. He still has specific fixations and will set his mind on something and it needs to be done right now. It seems like if he wants something, it's always something that is hard to get or not made anymore. He wanted one special book for his new baby sister and he had meltdowns over this book every day until it arrived at our house. Vio also still needs more breakthrough in academics and in comprehension of stories. He often revisits the past and will talk about random items that he used to see, like a red car driving by our old house. It's as if he's reconstructing the things he lost from the time when he was completely autistic.

We have seen the most amazing progress in the last five years that I have no doubt that God will continue to heal Vio and receive even more glory. I would be amazed for all my life even if nothing more would improve in the future, yet we know there is more. We continue to receive prophetic words about breakthrough and hold onto those. My husband and I have been proclaiming the things that the Lord has shown us for our kids and thanking God for the smallest things. We steward and celebrate every progress. In my heart, I feel that it is my holy task to claim everything Jesus has paid for at the cross for my son!

In my heart, I feel that it is my holy task to claim everything Jesus has paid for at the cross for my son!

A KEY FOR BREAKTHROUGH

CHRIS GORE

The day we met was unforgettable. For Jesus to speak "Eat bread and drink wine, and I will give you life" to a child who had no concept of communion reveals even more its importance to Him. The dreams that Vio had the two nights before we met were so powerful, but the timing of them was also personally significant. For years, I have been on a journey of going after an increase in revelation on the blood of Jesus; to greater understand how much the blood of Jesus paid for. Around just six months before meeting Vio was when I first preached a message at Bethel Church entitled, "The Power of the Lord's Table," sharing insights from the Lord on communion. So, when Vio said that the Lord gave him communion in his dream, it was significant.

Communion has had such a life-changing impact that now it has become a daily part of my life. We get to partake of it not out of tradition or religion, but as a daily act of remembering and recognizing the life and power that flows from Calvary. It is with a posture of humility and thanksgiving that we hold the bread and are grateful for His body that was broken so that we can walk in health. We do the same as we hold the juice as it reminds us not of our sin, but of the blood of Jesus that paid for the remission of all our sins: past, present, and future. The price of everything we need was paid for at the cross.

Our role is to continue to grow in understanding the significance of the Lord's body. In 1 Corinthians 11:29–30, it reads, "For he who eats and drinks in an unworthy manner, eats and drinks judgment to himself, not discerning the Lord's body. For this reason many are weak and sick among you, and many sleep."

"For this reason, many are weak and sick . . . " What reason is this Scripture pointing to? The answer is in the preceding verse, " . . . not discerning the Lord's body." Many would interpret this passage to mean that if you are unworthy, to not partake of communion. However, I want to propose that this passage is actually not about us at all. We are only unworthy apart from the blood of Jesus which is the whole reason for communion in the first place. It's not about us. It's about the blood of Christ and the price that Jesus paid for each one of us. What the writer Paul is saying is that the manner in which we take communion and discern the Lord's body will determine the benefits we experience. If our attitude is just that it's a piece of bread and grape juice, then that's what it will be and we will not fully experience the life-giving effects of the body and blood of Christ. There is healing available as we correctly discern the Lord's body.

Like I mentioned, we have an adult daughter who is disabled and who needs our full care. Only a few weeks before preaching that message on communion, I had a dream where I was giving her communion. She was unable to give it to herself, so needed it fed to her. As this was happening, the Lord spoke audibly in the dream, "Continue to discern My body." The dream flashed and the next image was her partaking communion by herself. I believe this was a picture of what happens when we correctly discern the Lord's body. We can come with an expectation that healing is going to flow!

REFLECTION #6

Find some time in your day to sit with Jesus and take communion with your child. Discern His body, His blood, and what happened at Calvary. Power and life flows through the sacrifice of Jesus! "This is My body which is given for you; do this in remembrance of Me." Luke 22:19

CHAPTER 5

PEACE RESTORED

TRUMAN'S STORY

When our son Truman was born, there was nothing to indicate to us that his journey of development would be different to his siblings. He was like every parent's dream—a nice, calm, sweet baby that would rest peacefully in my arms. However, around two months of age, we noticed that he was reacting to my breast milk and had an increased sensitivity to his diapers and clothes. Despite this, he continued to grow up quite well and even had good language development. Suddenly, all that changed when, around ten or eleven months of age, he lost all of his language skills. By the time he turned two, he was full of chaos and very angry. He would literally be angry from the time he woke up until the time he went to sleep. Since he no longer had words to communicate, he would scream instead. I found myself drowning in the chaos and anxiety. We knew something was wrong, so we sought out a specialized organization that would evaluate his development. They started doing their routine assessments and asked me specific questions about his abilities. Then, it hit me—he wasn't able to do anything that they were asking! They assessed him to be at a ten- to twelve-month developmental level at the age of two. I kept thinking, "No, this can't be so!" Once they left, I couldn't stop crying and searched on the internet for the signs of autism in a two-year-old. In that moment I realized that Truman had *every single one* of them.

Initially, I didn't seek an official diagnosis because I didn't want him to be labeled. So instead, I started pouring myself into learning how to naturally heal kids with autism. I put him on a special diet and supplements and saw a lot of progress. He started pointing with his finger and doing more things again. It was great to see my son emerge once again! We had worked hard with these changes, but then he hit a plateau. He quit progressing. There was still a lot of chaos and he didn't have receptive language skills. He wouldn't respond when I talked to him, wouldn't engage in joint attention or imaginative play, and also wouldn't play with toys appropriately. Going out in public was difficult for our family as he would melt down if there was too much stimulation or simply if he didn't like the feeling of his clothing on his skin.

I started realizing how I had done my part naturally and had put a lot of weight on that. I watched a video from Chris Gore about the peace of God referred to as "shalom." In that moment, the Lord tweaked my heart. He said, "I don't want you to stop doing the natural stuff, but I also don't want you to discount the supernatural stuff." I knew God was going to heal my son. The Lord had shown me Truman's potential even before he was born. I knew it was going to happen. It was a faith walk for me. I was living in God's promises of tomorrow while also living in the reality of today. It's like we were in two different time zones at the same time. I kept thinking, "I wish I had evidence of what I am hoping for" and then realized, "Oh, I do! That is faith! I have faith and that is my evidence because according to Hebrews 11:1, faith is the substance of things hoped for, the evidence of things not seen!"

Two weeks before Chris came in March of 2016, I made a video about the chaos that surrounded Truman. He would frequently "stim," which is where he would turn a lamp on the strobe-light setting, turn the music up as loud as it could go, and then begin jumping on the trampoline. It was the most chaotic thing! Then, a week before Chris came, we went to a testimony service at church where people were sharing about healings. I grabbed hold of all of these testimonies and prayed for accelerated healing for Truman. That week, he learned twenty-five new words such as cheek, tongue, thank you, his brother's name, up, milk, etc.! It was miraculous!

The next week Chris came to speak at our church. His belief is that the child is a perfect gift from God, but that the autism and the chaos they are trapped in is not. The simple prayer is this: "Shalom, the peace of God that breaks the chaos." We prayed that over Truman and let me tell you, he is walking in peace! The chaos is gone! The next day, my husband and I left on a much-needed trip and were gone for a week. His siblings got to watch his healing unfold and when we got home we couldn't believe it! Truman was not the same! His language really took off and even now, we continue to see daily improvements in his receptive language skills. He now gives hugs to people other than me, makes eye contact with others, engages with us as he shows us the new words he's learning, plays appropriately with toys, has imaginary play, waits patiently after communicating his requests, and is understanding us more when we give audible instructions! It used to be like he never even heard me when I would tell him to get his shoes, and now he does hear me and follows commands, which shows me that his auditory processing is better as well! As soon as he received prayer the spinning behaviors completely stopped too. He still likes the trampoline, but doesn't put on the chaotic music with strobe lights anymore! He used to freak out and cry for twenty minutes when we would change his clothes and now that is way easier! Also, before prayer, he had a ton of food allergies, but afterwards, five of them were instantaneously healed!

When Truman began getting the developmental assessments, I kept each and every one of them because I knew he would be healed and then I would have documentation of what God had done. Two days after Chris prayed for Truman, they came out to the house to do another assessment. The worker was touched, as that was his best assessment ever! She is a believer but didn't necessarily believe in healing as the norm. Afterwards, she told me, "I used to pray for the kids to just to be loved and accepted for who they are. This changes the way I pray!" Due to his age, Truman was going to be transitioning out of this program when he turned three a couple of weeks later. I love how God did it! I love that He broke in and showed off right before they stopped seeing him.

Truman is now four years old and is not completely on target verbally, but he is fading out of autism. He is bright and intelligent and has learned all of his letters even at a greater speed than his six-year-old sister. We pray over him every day and we pray specifically for how I've learned autism has affected his body. Truman even blesses his own body and tries to say some of the medical words. It is so cute, yet so powerful to teach him how to pray for himself. Our reality is that we did experience immediate healings after prayer and the chaos stopped, but that we are still walking it out. As many have asked about our story, I notice that so many people are afraid to hope. They say that if they hope, they will be disappointed. If we were really honest with ourselves, there are times we think that God is the God of disappointment. We say to ourselves, "I prayed. Something didn't happen, so therefore God must not answer our prayers." However, what we need to understand is that our God is Hope. He gives us the hope; He gives us the peace. Hope is the precursor to faith. Sometimes, it's hard to believe that Truman will ever be fully healed. However, my job is to tell myself, "No. There is hope. Don't you dare believe that lie!" As Truman has experienced healing and continues to do so, it always points back to Jesus as the One we can hope in.

Just as great as the progress that we've seen, we've also received an assurance that God is going to finish what He started! I know that Truman will be completely healed and will do great things. I know it's going to happen. My faith is the assurance that it will happen. I want to encourage you through a metaphor that God showed me. Picture a pie. Each slice of the pie represents aspects of God we can "eat" or take part in. There's a slice of healing, identity, prosperity, wholeness, or fill in the blank. Some think that just because one person is eating His "healing" slice, that it means they don't get to partake in that slice, as if there's only one pie for everyone to eat. Well guess what?! We each get a whole pie! If Truman is eating his slice of healing, you can too!

A KEY FOR BREAKTHROUGH

CHRIS GORE

Aren't we grateful that because of Jesus, we all get our own pie! Truman's mother described it so well in how Jesus has more than enough healing for everyone. Just as Jesus healed Truman of the extreme self-stimming behaviors and brought peace into their household, He has more than enough of that peace still available for everyone else. As Scripture tells us in Isaiah 9:6, Jesus is the Prince of Peace. Many families who have children with special needs can relate to the feelings of chaos described in this story. As precious as our children are, the stress and chaos can at times become over-whelming. Personally, we've had some really difficult times too, but be reminded again that the storm that may be *around* you, does not have to be *in* you!

In John 14:27, Jesus says, "Peace I leave with you, My peace I give you." The word "peace" in ancient Hebrew is "shalom," which when, studied further refers to the "spirit that destroys chaos." When you study the word "leave" in the original language, it means "bequest" which refers to the action of a rich person giving over his or her entire inheritance to someone. Knowing that, we can now read this passage as to say, "My peace, my shalom, my Spirit that destroys chaos, I leave and bequest all to you." Jesus has already given us the peace of Heaven!

We see this verse further come to life in the story recorded in Mark 4:35–41. The disciples are in a boat with Jesus during a storm. They've already seen some tremendous miracles, but they are freaking out in the boat and think that they are going to die. They wake up Jesus and He simply says to the storm, "Peace be still" and the storm is instantly calmed. I'd like to propose that Jesus was showing us that we can really only have authority over the storms of life that we can learn to rest in. Many of us are not in rest because we have so much turmoil, strife, fear, and chaos going on in our own life that it's pretty hard to create an environment of peace for our children. The peace that we carry as parents is transferable to our children and we can only give away what we know we've got. The second child we saw healed of autism actually happened after we laid hands on her mother and declared the shalom peace of Heaven over her first. The mother then went and prayed for her daughter and the daughter was healed! If we think about it, autism and any other sickness or condition is actually just chaos in our body. Thanks to Jesus, He has bequeathed to us His Spirit that destroys chaos!

Just as Jesus rested in the storm, we likewise can receive breakthrough as we learn to rest in the fire. The story of Shadrach, Meshach, and Abednego in the third chapter of Daniel illustrates this well. These men would not bow down in worship to idols that King Nebuchadnezzar had in place, so they were sentenced to be thrown into a fiery furnace. The fire was sent by the enemy to destroy them, not by God to refine them. We are told that the fire was heated up seven times hotter than normal and that the guards who put them in were instantly killed because of the intensity of the heat. Yet, Shadrach, Meshach, and Abednego were at a place of rest even in the fire. They were seen walking around, unbound and unharmed, with a fourth Person in the fire with them that looked like the Son of God. When we can keep our eyes on Jesus, the author and perfecter of faith (Hebrews 12:2), we can find rest even in the fire. Resting doesn't mean that we don't do anything. Rather, it means having an active trust that God is fighting on our behalf. The best thing we can do is to rest, knowing that the battle is not ours, it's the Lord's, and that He already won it on the cross. We simply get to watch and celebrate as the victory unfolds.

The most important and healthy thing for me and my family is that we stay in the peace of God no matter the circumstances. Remember that even in the midst of your enemies, He has prepared a table for you (Psalm 23:5). When you feel like you are in the fire, accept Jesus' invitation to feast and rest instead of partnering with fear and stress. When we can rest in the fire, we will not be burnt. With Shadrach, Meshach, and Abednego, the only things that got burnt off of them were the bondages that held them back from their destinies. God doesn't cause these fires in our lives, but be convinced that even in the midst of them, His peace is available and He is orchestrating your victory!

REFLECTION #7

Begin to daily declare the Shalom peace of Heaven over every circumstance in your family. Whether it is over your child's body or over your finances, God wants to calm the storms around you and bring restoration and healing. If you've lost your peace, reflect back on the moment in which it left and access again the presence of Holy Spirit, who is the Person of Peace that dwells inside of you.

CHAPTER 6

UNWAVERING TRUST

DAVID'S STORY

A s I was going about my morning routine, I heard God speak, "Are you going to trust Me no matter what today?" At the time, I was around fifteen weeks pregnant with my son. My response to God was "Of course I will trust You." For a faint moment, the thought that something could be wrong with my baby crossed my mind, but I quickly brushed it off and went about the rest of my morning to my doctor's appointment. It was there that I came face to face with the reality of why God had whispered that question to me earlier that day.

Before I can tell you the rest of our story, you must know the significance of trusting God for my son. Even before I was pregnant, I knew God had destined him for our family. One day, I was sitting in church and casually asked God about what boy name we should have if I ever became pregnant. Honestly I didn't expect Him to answer me, when all of a sudden, it was like everything went silent and black and I couldn't hear the pastor's words anymore. There it was . . . a flashing Vegas-like sign that read "David!" The flashing light was that of lightning striking and I heard the sound of thunder. It was so big, so bright, and so bold. There was no denying the name "*David*" and although David is my favorite person in the Bible, I honestly wanted a different name and knew that my husband would too. If it was truly the name that God had for my future son, He would have to convince us both. No sooner had I thought those words that I heard the name "Justin" in my spirit. Justin was the name of my brother-in-law. So I looked over at the soundboard where my husband was and whispered to him, "What is Justin's middle name?" To my surprise and shock, he mouthed back "David." I said to God, "I guess you have a David for us!"

So fast-forward to the day when God asked me if I was going to trust Him no matter what. I was around fifteen weeks pregnant and headed to the doctor as I had started leaking fluid. I was informed that a woman's amniotic sac would sometimes tear, but that it would simply repair on its own. However, we discovered that what we were dealing with was beyond repair. My sac had completely ruptured! There was absolutely no fluid left in the sac and babies need fluid to breathe and for their lungs to develop. There was no fluid and no way that I could get fluid inside to help my baby survive. Unless you've been there, you can't even imagine what it's like being told that your baby is not going to live. They couldn't understand how the baby was even still alive, but urged me to get an abortion. They said that my baby was going to die and not aborting could cause me to have an infection that would kill me as well.

I heard this devastating news and all I could think of is how God gave us the name "David" and then that morning asked me if I was going to trust Him no matter what I heard. So, we were living in the worst possible scenario and all I could say was, "God, I trust You." There was no way I would agree to an abortion. They tried to get an ultrasound to see the baby, but with a fluidless sac, only static appeared on the screen. I kept thinking that if I saw that my baby was a boy, I'd know that it was our David. After many weekly ultrasounds, finally God asked me, "Do you have to see that it's a boy to trust Me?" I said "no" and continued to trust Him through the process. No one wanted to treat me because they didn't agree with me keeping my baby as the risk of losing my life in the process was too great. Eventually, I found someone that would monitor us from home. I was on bed rest for eleven weeks and bled throughout the entire time. I would simply be sitting in my bed when all of a sudden I would get dizzy and blackout. When I would wake up, I would be paralyzed, in pain, and couldn't move for thirty minutes to an hour and then would bleed profusely throughout the rest of the night. Over the course of the eleven weeks, I had so many people coming over, praying, and speaking words of encouragement and life into our situation. Even amidst the grim prognosis, I continued to pray nonstop over my baby and declare every one of those prophetic words we had received.

Then the unimaginable happened. I had woken up in the middle of the night and made my way into the bathroom when I noticed a trail of blood from my bed to where I was standing. As I looked back at my bed, I saw that my entire mattress, including my pillow, was covered in blood. It was like a scene from a horror movie. My husband began screaming and my response was, "You have to hold it together for me!" I was afraid to go to the hospital because I knew that they would take my baby. Plus, I was only twenty-six weeks along at the time. However, at the same time, I knew it wasn't good. I immediately called my mom and we went to the hospital.

The look on people's faces said it all. Everyone kept looking at me as if saying with their eyes, "I'm so sorry." They could see that I probably had lost my baby. I was rushed in and everything was strapped to me to try to find my baby's heartbeat. At one point, the heartbeat started to go down and two nurses came in. They were watching me when all of a sudden, it went up and then six more people were surrounding my bed. That scene unfolded twice until in a moment it all stopped. The heartbeat went down and it wasn't coming up. I could hear in my periphery one of the nurses say, "I think we lost him." Then, there was the most beautiful noise a mother in this situation could hear. The beeping of her child's heartbeat again! All of the doctors and nurses screamed, "Go! Go!" and within seconds I was being prepped for a C-section. Within two minutes, I was already cut open. Everything was moving so quickly. I was nose-to-nose with my husband with his hands on my face. If he were to look away for

even a second, fear would overcome me and I would scream, "Look at me, look at me!" I remember barely seeing my baby as they whisked him away and ran. There was no pink to his little body; he was all so blue. I shouted to my husband to "Go" and he ran off with him.

I was placed alone in a dimly lit room to sit for awhile. My mom walked in and held her head low and couldn't even look me in the eyes. She was the one that through this whole thing was my champion and most positive; speaking prophetic words over me and my baby. When I saw her demeanor, it hit hard and I thought, "I lost the one person who had all the hope in the world." I felt devastated. A nurse followed in after her with the repeated phrase of "I'm so sorry, I'm so sorry." All I could think of was that I needed to see my baby.

They wheeled me in and I still couldn't see him through the six or seven doctors who were surrounding his bed working on him. Everyone, including my husband, had their heads down. The doctor turned to me and said, "I'm sorry, but we need to pull the plug. We are hurting him by trying to keep him alive. He has had no oxygen to his brain for awhile and he's completely brain dead. There's bleeding in the brain and spine and he's not really alive. We are just trying to keep his heart going." All I kept thinking was "God, you're not a liar! God, you're not a liar!" I told them I needed to talk to my husband and please not to give up! They wheeled me into the next room where my parents waited. At the time, my husband worked at the hospital and his worst fear was having a child as a "vegetable." "We can't have a vegetable. We can't do this to him," was my husband's response.

I responded, "God doesn't lie! He doesn't lie! He said David! He told me to trust Him!" For a minute I felt this confusion come on me and I questioned if my son would die. If he died, that would mean that everything that I believed in was not true. So I said "No".

We were fighting back and forth desperately pleading with each other when my dad stepped in. He said, "Let's stop for a second and pray." The moment my dad started praying, you could feel Holy Spirit come into the room. I remember the way I begged for my son's life. In that moment, I could relate to the scene in the Bible when Jesus was sweating blood. I felt like my body was going to die by the way I was contending and pleading for my kid's life. I begged God and started declaring every promise I heard when I was pregnant and declaring that God is not a liar. As we were praying, all of a sudden I got this urge that I needed to touch him. During this time, twice the nurse came in and was crying and said, "I'm so sorry for your loss." I yelled to her to not let the doctors give up!

They wheeled me out there again but this time all of the doctors were standing back. They were waiting for him to pass. Because I couldn't sit up after the surgery, I was only able see his little foot which was blue and the size of a quarter. He was only a pound and a half and 11.5 inches. He was so tiny. The lack of fluid made it so he couldn't grow or develop his lungs in utero. I put my finger and thumb over his little, blue foot and started praying in the Spirit. I'm sure all the doctors were wondering what was going on. Everyone stood behind me completely quiet. For around five minutes, I was pleading for David's life.

The rest of the forty-five minutes was just thanking God and praising Him. I thought to myself, "This is odd. They said my kid is pretty much dead and I am thanking You, God." I kept praising Him and praying in the Spirit when all of a sudden, my mom leaned her head next to mine and quietly said, "His chest just sank in like he took a breath!" I kept praying and she again whispered to me, "He's turning pink." I looked at her, gave her a little smile, but was not done yet. I kept praying and praying until his chest moved again. He took two breaths!

> *I kept praising Him and praying in the Spirit when all of a sudden, my mom leaned her head next to mine and quietly said, "His chest just sank in like he took a breath!"*

They pushed me aside and started hooking him up to everything. His specialist, who was top in his field and had even been on the cover of magazines, came over to speak to us. He said, "In all my twenty-five years of practice, I've never seen a kid like this. I can't give you a diagnosis or tell you what to even expect because I've never had a baby survive this." Wisdom hit me in that moment. I felt in my heart that this was going to be a journey, so when he said those things, I told God, "Okay, the ball is in your court. I trust you." I was told that he would probably not make it through the night and that if by chance he did, he would be completely brain dead. He survived the night and when they did a brain scan the next day, it showed just a little bit of dried blood at his brain stem. They couldn't believe it! There was nothing wrong with his brain! After months in the hospital and against all odds, we finally got to take our baby David home!

There are moments when I would be reminded of the fear that still remained in my heart in regard to David's life. Even after going home, his lungs still looked like spiderwebs on the x-rays and he had chronic lung disease for a couple of years with multiple hospital stays. When he was one year old, we noticed that his head looked like it was swelling. The doctors did a scan and said that there was fluid building on his brain and that emergency surgery may be needed. I fell apart. After all he had made it through, I didn't realize that I still had so much fear that he would die. In that moment, one of my friends prayed the simplest prayer over us: "Jesus, I just ask that when they look at the scans in the morning, they will notice that there was no fluid at all." I saw it as a nice, even cute prayer, but honestly, I didn't have a lot of faith for that to actually be our reality. I didn't sleep that night as we waited for the phone call the next morning about his surgery. The phone rang and I heard a voice on the other end telling me, "I don't know what we were looking at yesterday, but there is no fluid on his brain." He didn't need surgery after all! That simple prayer was answered exactly the way she asked! I was reminded yet again of when God asked me if I would trust Him.

When David was around three years old, differences in his development and behavior became more and more apparent and the specialists started talking about the diagnosis of autism. However, he was still seen as a mystery and there were so many different opinions as to his actual diagnosis. Some specialists said autism while others said he was in his own category due to the lack of oxygen he experienced. I simply called it autism because it was easier to explain to people. His life began with specialists and continued to be filled with appointments for physical therapy, speech therapy, occupational therapy, vision exams, and follow-ups with the lung- and brain doctors. Like a lot of families who have a child with special needs, all of these demands can take a toll on your family life. There were definitely rocky times throughout this journey of constant faith. I watched my husband cave and not be able to handle life anymore. One day, it all became too much for him and he left; leaving me as a single mom to David who just turned four and his sister, only three months. A couple of months later, I packed my kids in the car and we decided to start a new chapter in our lives and pursue healing for David in Redding, California.

Our journey at Bethel Church began by going to the Healing Rooms every Saturday. At that time, they didn't yet have a special-needs Sunday-school classroom so the Healing Rooms became church to me. So for several hours every Saturday morning, we would just soak in the presence of God. It was and still is my sacred place and most precious time. Their team of children would minister to us and others would pray for me and speak prophetic words over our family. They would agree with me for David's healing. It was what we all needed! Just during those months of being in God's presence in the Healing Rooms was when David was finally potty trained! Tangible breakthrough was beginning to happen right before our eyes! Also during that time, I heard a teaching by the Healing Rooms Director, Chris

Gore, on speaking Shalom peace over children with autism and how many children had been healed. I sought him out and ever since that day, if David is having an episode and freaking out, I simply put my two hands on his head and whisper "Shalom," and he slowly turns into jello and doesn't move. Peace is restored to him in those moments.

When David was five years old, my prayers were answered and Bethel started a special-needs classroom on Sundays called "Breakthrough." It was like a normal Sunday school class, but with both children's ministry workers and Healing Rooms volunteers who pray for the children. I was so scared to drop him off for the first time. For his entire life, I had never left his side, even for a minute. I couldn't even shower for his first year of life without the shower curtain open because he would pull off his oxygen and his lips would turn blue. For the first time in five years, I left him and was able to go to church! I thank God that he loved it! It was right around that time that David started experiencing more healing and had several more firsts! He finally said his first word, which was "Mama" and took his first bite of solid foods! He was progressing more and more! Also, for the first time, he looked me in the eyes. There's no feeling like it when you experience another level of heart connection and communication with your child! Sometimes now, he will come close to me and just look at me. He thinks it's so funny when people smile because when they do, their eyes change shape, like an arc. So now, he will put his face right in front of my face, look me in the eyes, and say "arc eyes" to make me smile, then continue to belly laugh.

Over the years, I have learned to recognize the different ways in which Jesus ministers to my son. I have always wanted to know what David was thinking, especially when he wasn't talking as much as he is now. One of the common words that I heard from people was that he gets ministered to in the middle of the night. When he was in the incubator for four months, I would stay there all day long and before going home at night, I would always ask God to minister to him during the night and to have angels sing and play with him. Every single night when he came home from the hospital until he was a couple years old, he would wake up and belly laugh for sometimes up to an hour. To this day, he will still sometimes wake up during the night and laugh hysterically. He doesn't really tell me too much about what happens at night, but recently, he woke up and told me, "Jesus was on my tummy." I don't know exactly what that meant, but I know it's God encountering him. Another time when we were in the Healing Rooms, three different people told me that Jesus ministers to David through his stuffed Mickey Mouse. Every day he would hold Mickey nose-to-nose and talk to him. I would see David holding Mickey nose-to-nose and hear him repeatedly say "Oh, my boy. Oh, I love you so much." I always thought David was saying that to Mickey until I had an encounter with God that changed how I saw David's interactions. One day, I was walking through the living room and from out of nowhere, I felt the embrace of Jesus. I felt Him wrap His arms around me from behind and He said to me, "Oh, my girl. Oh, I love you so much." I realized in that moment, that maybe it wasn't that David was talking to Mickey. David most often would repeat what he was hearing, so I believe he was repeating to Mickey what he was hearing from the Father! God was encountering my son and speaking love over him through his Mickey Mouse!

Even though he's still slowly progressing, he's such a different kid than a couple of years ago that it impresses his teachers and specialists too! One day, I was in the house and called out, "David, where are you?" Normally, he will just grunt or yell, never answering me back. That day, I called out to him and he said, "I'm in the kitchen." I gasped and just started crying. David had answered me! It may not seem like a big deal for most people, but he answered me! It was significant breakthrough and he's answering me more and more in this way. I also remember one morning heading to his Sunday school class when David was fussy and kept saying, "tummy." I responded with tears yet again. David could be bleeding from the head and he would never cry or show any sign of distress to me. He'd just go lay in his bed. It was the first time he let me know he was uncomfortable! To never knowing when your kid is hurting, to finally seeing breakthrough of him being able to express discomfort; I was overcome with joy.

David used to be constantly over-stimulated and upset, but now it's more common for him to giggle and laugh instead. He is incredibly smart and can say his ABCs forward and backward in three different languages. He learned how to count in five languages, including sign language, simply by watching it once or twice on YouTube. Because he doesn't understand certain things, he'll surprise and blow everyone away with something that he completely comprehends in a way most adults can't

even do. The most recent development is that his teachers and I learned at the same time that he could not only perfectly tune a ukulele, but could also perfectly play the hymn, "Joyful, Joyful, We Adore Thee." In David fashion, he just grabbed the ukulele one day at Sunday school and started playing it flawlessly. We were all amazed!

Within months of first being in his Sunday school class, he was leaving Mickey behind and talking to the adults, something he never would do before. He now interacts with them with full sentences and acknowledges and talks to other kids in the classroom. For the first time in the two years that he's been going there, he started eating snacks and asked the teacher to play catch with him. They love him there so much and are blown away with the healing that Jesus has done and is continuing to do!

David's eyes have also experienced some healing as well. Because he was on so much oxygen when he was born, his vision is extremely compromised. The doctors said that neither glasses nor surgery would correct the problem. That was okay with me as it was another ball to be put in God's court that only He could fix. One day I looked at David's eyes and they weren't crossing like they had been before! He still looks at things a couple of inches away from his face and when he's tired, his eyes will cross a little bit, but they are not crossed as much as they used to be!

It is so touching to hear about how he ministers to other children as well. His Sunday school teacher said that one day, he wanted to be rocked in a blanket. She was holding one end of the blanket and the other teacher was helping a child who was blind hold the other end. As they rocked back and forth, suddenly David looked up at the other child and exclaimed, "Eyes." He wasn't close enough to her to see that she was blind, and at that point, he had never interacted with her to know that. In his own way, he was declaring healing over her. Then, just recently, he was in class with a young adult who has cerebral palsy and doesn't talk or walk. He was so happy to see her and kept telling her "Hi." He then walked up to her and kept repeatedly saying, "Talk to me. Talk to me." Even though he genuinely wanted to talk with her, which is a miracle in and of itself that he is seeking out social interactions, it was also a declaration of healing! He also now picks up on my social cues. He can always tell when I'm a little on edge and he thinks it's funny. He will come up to me, start poking at me, and pull me right out of what I'm feeling!

Throughout this journey, I continue to hold onto hope for David's continued healing. He has come so far and I know God isn't finished yet. I continue to declare the things that I want to see happen. My son is going to be able to see me from across the room! He is going to communicate his heart to me! He's going to be able to articulate his thoughts and emotions even better! I feel like he will always be unique and a little mystery to us all, but I know one day, we will be able to talk and laugh like I can with my daughter. In the meantime, I will simply continue to trust God no matter what!

He has come so far and I know God isn't finished yet.

A KEY FOR BREAKTHROUGH

ANGELA LOCKE

Te•na•cious // Persistent in maintaining, adhering to, or seeking something valued or desired; persistence, determination, perseverance, resolve, steadfastness, endurance.

If there is one word to describe David's mom, it is "tenacious." Her resolve to take Jesus at His word is the type that will see mountains move and has reignited faith and hope in so many people. It is a fierce type of faith. It's the type that knows the goodness of God, yet wrestles with Him and refuses to let go until the fullness of His kingdom comes. There is no doubt that David's doctors still feel the impact of her faith when they see that he not only survived, but also is thriving more than ever expected!

I met David and his family around three years ago in the Bethel Healing Rooms and then subsequently as he became one of the first children in our Sunday school class for children with special needs. There are no words to adequately describe the change that we all see in him. It is remarkable and brings us to tears. Every day that he comes to our classroom is a reminder of the healing power and grace of Jesus. Jesus is truly incredible and we are seeing more and more of David emerge!

There is a place in God's heart where you can access this tenacity. It is part of His nature to be tenacious, so as a believer you have access to this too. Daily, the Father exudes this quality as He pursues His creation with an unwavering love and steadfast desire. Throughout my own journey of multiple losses in my family and personal disappointments, it has been the Father's tenacity, love, and grace that has marked my life the most. Difficult moments happen in life, but what matters is what we choose to do with them and how we allow them to affect our heart, theology, and walk with the Lord. Our circumstances do not define Him, but they will define us in whatever way we give them permission to. When the storms of life come, run deep into the Father's heart. We need to come to a place where we abide in Him in such a way that all of the trials and questions fade as we only become increasingly aware of His great love towards us. He is your hiding place and your shield! (Psalm 119:114).

One of my favorite heroes in the Bible is Abraham. In Romans 4, we read about his great faith. Here Abraham has a really big promise from God that he would become the father of nations, yet he doesn't even have one child yet. To top that off, his wife Sarah is barren and he is around a hundred years old and the Bible says that he recognized that his body was "as good as dead." That doesn't sound like hopeful odds at all! Yet, in verses 18-21 in the English Standard Version, we are infused with tenacity as we read: "In hope he [Abraham] believed against hope, that he should become the father of many nations . . . No unbelief made him waver concerning the promise of God, but he grew strong in his faith as he gave glory to God, fully convinced that God was able to do what He had promised."

Wow, that stirs my heart! This specific version states that he grew strong in his faith *as* he gave glory to God. This emphasizes that giving thanks for the promises spoken over our lives is a key to helping us actually grow in faith until they come to pass. God fulfilled His promise to Abraham and he became the father of many nations! Get alone with Jesus and wait there until you are fully convinced that God is able to perform His words over you life. Give Him glory both in the midst of joy and also while waiting for the full manifestation of the promise, and like David's mom did when she touched his little foot that day in the incubator . . . don't let go. He is and will always be the God of the impossible! He is faithful to His word!

REFLECTION #8

There are things that we all have prayed and contended for, even for months and years. Recently, God reminded me that He is answering prayers that we don't even pray any longer. Take a moment to thank God for still holding in faith what we may have left behind in hopelessness. Ask Him to reignite your prayer life and to give you tenacious hope for those very things that are dear to your heart.

REFLECTION #9

Just as David's mom knew that God had promised her a son, there are promises that God has for all of us. You can find many in Scripture and others that He has personally written on your heart. Take time to write out both types of promises and keep them in a place where you can see them and remember what He has spoken over your life.

CHAPTER 7

STEWARDING THE MIRACULOUS

KENDRA'S STORY

Kendra is our 23-year-old wonderful daughter. She was born three months premature and contracted a virus that led to her becoming deaf at eight months. She was also diagnosed as legally blind, developmentally delayed, and autistic. In 2002, it was discovered that she had a tethered cord and needed surgery on her spine. As a result of that surgery, she apparently had some permanent nerve damage and became incontinent and would wet the bed. Her problem came and went over the past twelve years, but in 2011, Kendra's bedwetting started to increase both in intensity and frequency to where by Christmas of 2012 her wetting was at least six nights a week for many months. We were at a loss and becoming increasingly frustrated and Kendra's self-esteem was at an all-time low. In 2013, we took Kendra to a naturopath to help us brainstorm and find natural ways to change her diet and see if acupuncture might help with the bedwetting. Although we saw some improvements from that, Kendra still did not experience complete breakthrough and she would go through seasons of wetting 4–5 times a week after many months of treatment.

Several years before this, a friend who knew of some of our many struggles with Kendra mentioned Healing Rooms to me. He told me about ones he'd heard about in Spokane in the '50s and '60s. At the time I was not quite ready to embrace such a concept and though I was intrigued, I filed that thought away for almost six years. In 2015, I had heard about Pastor Bill Johnson and early one Sunday morning, I could not sleep and started watching Bill on YouTube. It was a powerful message and at the end of it he mentioned that Bethel Church loved to pray for healing. Bill's invitation was sincere and God spoke to me in that moment and reminded me that I needed to take Kendra to a healing room—somewhere. Bethel seemed a bit far, but the compulsion was so strong that I emailed my friend, hoping that he could connect me with any healing room in our area. As it was still very early in the morning, I was not expecting a reply from him any time soon.

My phone rang within a minute of sending off the email and it was my friend calling me. I told him about the message by Bill and asked about Spokane and then if he knew anything about Bethel Church and their healing rooms. Before he could answer, I asked why he was up so early on a Sunday morning. He said they were just coming back from Bethel that very morning! They were getting ready to leave for the long drive back up to Portland right when he got my email on his phone. I was stunned and decided then and there to email Bethel church to ask about what arrangements could be made for sign-language services. Later that morning, we went to our home church and after service I asked a woman, who I considered gifted in the prophetic, for prayer for wisdom if we should make the trip. I

told her about the email with my friend. She began laughing and stated that she and her husband just got back from Bethel last week themselves! She said that they actually make the trip down to Bethel every few months. I asked her why, and she told me about a miraculous relieving of chronic knee pain when her son and his friend came home from Bethel School for Christmas break. I was undone by this point as within four hours of each other, I had confirmation from two different people who did not know each other who were not only aware of Bethel, but were frequent visitors specifically for healing. Needless to say, I knew at that point we needed to go. We talked it over with Kendra and she was excited to go and be healed!

Our visit to the Healing Rooms was everything we could have hoped for and yet completely unexpected. We met up with the lead sign-language interpreter for Bethel who had already arranged for not only two sign-language interpreters so Kendra could take in as much of the worship and healing as possible, but also a whole team of intercessors to pray specifically for Kendra and her many needs. We were overwhelmed by it all. The intercessory team prayed over Kendra and the interpreters were signing the entire time. They prayed not only for the incontinence, but also for the autism and low vision and pretty much every challenge she has faced. It was truly remarkable and the ministry touched all of us.

When we woke up the next morning, there was great news. Kendra had been dry all night! Other than the first night dry in a long time, another thing out of the ordinary we noticed was in Kendra's reaction to the many deaf people who came up to greet her at the signing service that next morning. Normally, Kendra's autism doesn't show up around hearing people, but around the deaf. Since she only uses American Sign Language (ASL), hearing people don't seem to upset her and she does not present strong autistic behaviors around them since she knows she will not need to talk with them. However, we've noticed that around deaf people, her autism presents itself more strongly since there is an expectation for more social interaction. In the past, had she been surrounded by so many unknown deaf people who came up to greet her in ASL, she would have freaked. We sat watching how she handled that situation and she seemed much more poised than we'd seen before and her interactions were very appropriate. As several of the deaf elders gathered around her to pray, she was simply beaming.

> *When we woke up the next morning, there was*
> *great news. Kendra had been dry all night!*

As we began the drive home, one of Kendra's first questions was about when we could come back. We got home exhausted and yet feeling full of promise. As Kendra got ready for bed that night, we simply gathered to thank the Lord for getting us down to Bethel, for the prayers for healing, and for whatever the Lord would do from that point forward. The next morning Kendra was dry again! She was so happy. She was then dry the next night, and the next. By three weeks of steady dry nights, Kendra

went to her room, took all of the pads and plastic sheets off of her bed, and put them in the middle of the living room floor and signed to her mom, "I'm done. I'm healed." She went seven straight weeks without bedwetting and she hadn't done that in six years!

As you can see in the below screenshot, just ten days after our visit to Bethel, Kendra had a follow-up appointment in which her doctor documented that "She has been dry dry dry recently."

SUBJECTIVE

She has been dry dry dry recently. Very thrilled about this.

(This was just after our first visit to the Bethel healing room on 8/21/2015. To us, this seven week period where she wet not once in that time, was a miracle.)

Seven weeks after this healing, Kendra started having occasional bedwetting again. I began rereading the teaching notes from the Bethel Healing Rooms about stewarding your healing. The part that stood out to me was how God will provide the healing, but how He wants us to steward what He has done and take ownership. We talked with Kendra, and it turned out that she was getting lax with some habits that were likely contributing to her problem. When she got healed of the bedwetting, she didn't have the internal/mental insights to know how to maintain it. It was as if she felt that now that she was healed, she could just relax. So every night, we began to pray wisdom over her and she can internalize this concept now! She had to take ownership and she ended up realizing that this was possible! She is now dry 98% of the time, with the other percent only happening during her monthly cycle. It is a predictable pattern that we can now address. After years of this being almost a daily struggle for her, we are so delighted that she is free from it!

Though this was a major breakthrough for Kendra, a perhaps even bigger one started to become evident since we first observed Kendra interact with the deaf worshipers at Bethel during our visit. One of Kendra's caregivers in Portland, who has known Kendra since kindergarten, made a comment not long after we returned from Bethel that Kendra seemed far more interactive at the deaf social functions. Previously, Kendra would tend to be off by herself with very limited interaction. As of late, she noted that Kendra would seek out other deaf people she knew and that her poise and comfort level and social interactions overall were markedly changed. Remembering that the prayer team also prayed for healing of autism, it appeared that it too was now being impacted. This came to a much fuller realization when Kendra asked to go on a deaf missions trip to a Christian Deaf School in Mexico. The thought of Kendra going on this trip without one of her parents seemed inconceivable to us both, much less that she would want to do such a thing. Nevertheless, she was very determined to go, and after several meetings with the deaf team going down, she committed to the trip and all we can say is praise God! This truly was miraculous in that before prayer, such a trip would not have been at all possible for Kendra for several reasons, not the least of which was the autism which would have held her back from even wanting to go. We've not had Kendra re-assessed for autism, as it would be hard to completely separate out all of the various factors. However, in our opinion, having lived with Kendra these 24 years, she seems much more fulfilled, involved, and socially aware than before the power of healing prayer. Our faith has increased by leaps and bounds and we have been telling as many other parents of special-needs kids about what we have experienced and that there is not only hope but healing as well to be found in the most unlikely places.

We can't wait to see what God is going to do next in our lives. Kendra has even started to self-report pain, which is new for her. We've seen that God is always doing something as we've embraced the process. Kendra has a touch on her life where so many people have learned and benefitted through her. It used to be a lot about us, as we were just in survival mode. Now, however, it's different. We pray and the Lord gives all of us, including Kendra, insights that in turn help other people. All glory to Jesus! He is good!

There is not only hope but healing as well to be found in the most unlikely places.

A KEY FOR BREAKTHROUGH

CHRIS GORE

The healing power of Jesus is incredible to witness. However, do you know that healing is not God's best? It's actually walking in divine health all the days of your life. There's nothing more heartbreaking to see people get radically touched and healed by God to only hear months later that they are again struggling with the same symptoms as before. Jesus is the Healer, not the un-healer. He doesn't heal someone and then take it back if they have a less-than-perfect day. He gives good gifts and they are given without repentance. So if there is a return of symptoms, where is the disconnect? I propose that it's actually in the process of stewardship. In Kendra's story, she had received healing and then experienced a temporary regression. During this time, she realized that she had stopped doing things in the natural that had contributed to her breakthrough. It was through the revelation of stewardship and co-laboring with God, naturally and supernaturally, that she regained and maintained her breakthrough.

Years ago, it was the night before a speaking engagement and thoughts about this topic were on my mind. That night, I had a dream where the Lord spoke audibly and gave me six specific points on stewarding healing. This book is full of many of those keys, but in this chapter we will briefly expound on three of them that particularly relate to Kendra's story.

The first point is very practical. In 1 Corinthians 6:19, it says that our bodies are the temple of the Holy Spirit. So, how are we taking care of His temple? It's important that we care for our bodies the best that we can. Just like being forgiven doesn't give us a license to sin, so it is that being healed doesn't give us a license to do whatever we want to our bodies. We always live under grace, but within that grace comes responsibility. Understanding grace should make us desire to live righteously as should being made well make us desire to live healthy lives. If we're not responsible for what we receive, we may eventually lose it. Eating healthy, exercising, and treating our bodies well unto the Lord are all acts of worship. In this practical stewardship, remember that our Redeemer is still Jesus. Our faith is in the faith of Christ and is not in broccoli or cauliflower. Kendra realized what her role was in the natural stewardship of her body and regained victory!

The second point is to not play the shame game. It could've been so easy for Kendra and her family to partner with shame when the regression happened. When someone has publicly shared about their healing and then symptoms return, shame and guilt may try to come in. The person may not even go back for prayer and may stop sharing with others about their breakthroughs. We've all heard the saying, "Shame on you." Well, we say, "Shame off you!" We want to encourage you, if regression happens, come back to the source of healing who is Jesus. Celebrate in everything that Jesus has done. He really did something miraculous and no one can take that breakthrough moment away. Keep looking to Jesus, praying, and rejoicing!

Last, but certainly not least, is to remember that even as we co-labor with Jesus, healing is all by His grace. In John 19:30, Jesus' last words on the cross were, "It is finished." At the cross, everything changed. The law was fulfilled and we are no longer under law; we are under God's grace. If we don't think that healing is by His grace, we will always refer back to law to be healed or formulas in order to retain our healing. He took what we deserve, so that we can receive what He deserved! Do your part, but remember to rest in His grace!

REFLECTION #10

Stewardship is so important. It looks like taking care of our bodies in the natural, trusting God to do the supernatural, as well as remembering and celebrating what He has done. Ask Holy Spirit to show you what His idea of stewardship looks like for your family's life in this season and write it down. What He reveals, He also gives grace to see come to pass.

REFLECTION #11

As the last reflection in this book, ask Holy Spirit to show you how to personally steward what you have received from reading all of these stories. Share what He says with someone close to you who can continue to spur you on in this walk of faith.

CONCLUSION

Our journeys in life are all so different, yet so valuable. In speaking with each of these families, we intentionally honored and celebrated each family's process. Whether we had doctor's notes verifying the healing or simply listened to a family where their child had what may have seemed like a smaller change, it all mattered to us and to Heaven. Wherever you find yourself or your family on this journey, I want to encourage you to find your contentment, hope, and joy in Jesus alone. Our contentment in life cannot come only when we get a miracle. We have been praying for our daughter since she was born, and have made the conscious decision to live in a place of contentment and stay in the present. Joy is an "inside job" and is something that we cannot allow our outside circumstances to define. Do difficult times still happen in our family? Yes. However, in the midst of those times, we look to find where Jesus is in our situation. He is always there.

In the introduction, there was a story about when Kris Vallotton spoke directly into my life during a hard season that we were having with Charlotte. During that conversation, I had also said to him that I really didn't feel like I was living much of a life at the moment. His response to me was, "Chris, this is your life right now. What if the miracle doesn't come? Will you lead the rest of your life unhappy?" This wasn't a statement of unbelief but rather one of perspective. My contentment cannot be based on if Charlotte had a seizure today or not, but rather in Jesus Christ and Him alone. I've taught this all over the world, but there was another layer of fresh revelation that unfolded that day. In those moments where our world feels like it's in a tailspin, all we need to do is stop, take a breath, speak peace over ourselves, and find Jesus in that moment. Our family is going to live the best, happy life we can right now, and stay in place of contentment, hope, and joy, as we trust Jesus with the future.

Stories like the ones in this book move our hearts, but they do so much more than that. They release tangible faith and hope and also prophesy to our own destinies as well. In Revelation 19:10b, the Bible states, "The testimony of Jesus is the spirit of prophecy." This means that every testimony that we have ever heard, including those in the Bible, carries the power of the Holy Spirit to do it again! Every word of hope and healing that you have just read prophesies for the same to be available in your life! We believe that many will experience the healing power of Jesus just by reading these words and would love to hear about the breakthroughs that you and your family experience!

We trust that you have been filled with hope and encouragement as you have read this writing. Our heart's desire and goal is that worldwide, every parent or grandparent of a child with special needs would receive a copy of this book for free. If this book has impacted you, we'd like to invite you to pay it forward by purchasing a book for us to give to another family. We would be able to put this in the hands of families anywhere in the world for an average $34.95 USD per book (which includes shipping).

For questions or to join us in this exciting endeavor, please email us or send your gift directly, noting it as "Seeding a book," to the following PayPal address: ThePerfectGiftProject@gmail.com

In conclusion, let's pray:

Jesus,

We thank You for every person reading this book and ask that they will have a tangible encounter with Your goodness and grace. We release hope and faith to come upon each member of their household in a greater measure and speak Shalom peace to every circumstance and condition. May You, Jesus, be glorified and get Your full reward! Amen

VIDEOS AND RESOURCES

To access any of the below resources, you can download a free QR code scanner on your smart device or some devices allow you to simply use your photo app and point it at the QR code to open it. Alternatively, you can go directly to

www.chrisgore.org

BETHEL'S BAPTISM FOR CHILDREN WITH SPECIAL NEEDS

During Bethel's Sunday morning services, we have a ministry for children with special needs. One of the children asked to be baptized, so we set up a special time that would be more sensory-sensitive and baptized eleven children. Some of them were afraid of the water and some of them didn't want to get out, but there was plenty of grace to meet the children exactly where they were. It was one of our most beautiful and unique baptism services. What a blessing it was to witness the simplicity of their faith and to be a part of their continued journey into healing. Scan the following code to be taken to the video and prepare for your heart to be melted!

Bethel's Baptism for Children with Special Needs

VIDEO TEACHINGS AND PRIVATE FACEBOOK GROUP FOR PARENTS OF CHILDREN WITH SPECIAL NEEDS

Some of the material in this book was adapted from five video teachings that were developed out of the conversations that I've often had with parents. In addition, there is a private Facebook group called "Healing is the Children's Bread" designed for parents and caregivers of children with special needs who have a heart to pursue healing for their children. It's a place of encouragement where parents can both pray for each other and celebrate in each other's victories. We weren't meant to do this journey alone! Scan the below codes to be taken directly to these resources. May you find encouragement, hope, and faith in your journey of healing!

Video 1 – The Perfect Gift

Video 2 – No Offense Taken

Video 3 – Celebrate the Small

Video 4 - Contentment in Jesus

Video 5 - The Peace of Heaven

"Healing is the Children's Bread"
Facebook Group

Follow Chris on Facebook
www.facebook.com/ChrisGoreNZ

–

Share your testimony with us at ThePerfectGiftProject@gmail.com

OTHER BOOK TITLES BY CHRIS GORE:

-

Walking in Supernatural Healing Power

Practical Guide to Walking in Healing Power

Overflow: A Daily Experience of Heaven's Abundance

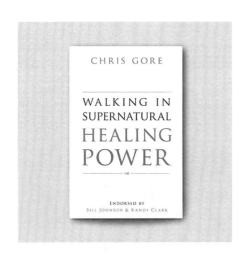

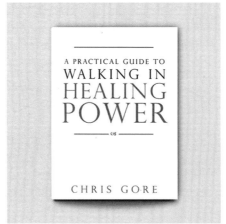